A First Home Economics Course

Also available from Stanley Thornes (Publishers) Ltd:

A Practical Guide to Child Development Volume 1: The Child
Valda Reynolds

A Practical Guide to Child Development Volume 2: The Family
Valda Reynolds

A Practical Guide to Child Development Teacher's Book
Valda Reynolds (Publication due late 1987)

A First Home Economics Course

Valda Reynolds Cert.Ed.
Joint Chief Examiner, Midland Examining Group, for GCSE Home Economics: Child Development

Glenys Wallis Cert. Ed. Home Economics

Stanley Thornes (Publishers) Ltd

First published in 1987 by:
Stanley Thornes (Publishers) Ltd
Old Station Drive
Leckhampton
CHELTENHAM GL53 0DN
England

British Library Cataloguing in Publication Data

Reynolds, V.
A first home economics course.
1. Home economics
I. Title   II. Wallis, G.
640   TX167

ISBN 0-85950-675-4

Typeset by Tech-Set, Gateshead, Tyne & Wear in 11/13 Palatino.
Printed and bound in Great Britain at The Bath Press, Avon.

Contents

Preface   vii

Acknowledgements   ix

Introduction   **Family Life and Healthy Living**   1
                    Family life   1
                    Healthy living for the family   4

Section One   **Health and Body Maintenance**   5
                    Taking exercise   5
                    Fresh air   21
                    Sleep   23
                    Stress   27
                    Body abuse   30
                    Personal cleanliness   39
                    Mental attitudes   51

Section Two   **Health and Safety**   54
                    Accidents in the home   54
                    Causes and prevention of accidents   55
                    Road safety   64
                    Safety at school   78
                    Safety at work   80
                    Safety at play   82
                    Safety on the water   84
                    People and organisations who look after our safety   87
                    Safety and the law   88
                    First aid   91

Section Three	**Health and Food**	**96**
	A healthy varied diet	96
	Choosing food	96
	Nutritional value	98
	Dietary goals	102
	Eating patterns	103
	Family meals	110
	Buying and storage	116
	Consumer information	121
	Food additives	125
Section Four	**Health and Dress**	**127**
	Fashion	**127**
	History	128
	Personality	134
	Colour	136
	Style	138
	Fabric	140
	Fashion buying	140
	Accessories	142
	Dress sense	144
	Types of fabric	146
	Fibres to yarns to fabrics	148
	Properties and special finishes	153
	Fabrics for a purpose	157
	Dress care	158
	Choosing	159
	Wearing	160
	Cleaning	160
	Storing	164
	Repairing	166
	Conclusion	**171**
	Glossary	**173**
	Index	**175**

Preface

A FIRST HOME ECONOMICS COURSE is designed to provide a foundation course in Home Economics for girls and boys in middle school and the first years of secondary school, and a useful basic information guide for examination work. The theme is 'Family life and healthy living' and the book is divided into four sections:

Health and Body Maintenance
Safety
Food
Dress

These sections give information on some of the major aspects and unifying themes defined in the National Criteria for Home Economics.

The information is presented in an up-to-date and lively manner which will interest and stimulate the pupil. The text is clear and easily understood by this age range. It is interspersed with a wide range of diagrams, charts, drawings and suggestions for activities. These will encourage the pupil to seek out further information, observe, record and then assess and evaluate given situations – all of which are assessment objectives relating to the National Criteria.

Communication skills are developed by suggested topics for group debate – the 'Discussion Areas'.

The old fashioned 'stitching and stirring' idea of Home Economics has been replaced by:

- up-to-date scientific theories
- the latest nutritional theories based on NACNE
- a non-sexist approach
- integration of practical and theoretical ideas.

Each section is sub-divided into several topics (see contents list) each of which can be used by the teacher as a self-contained unit for a piece of class work or for separate pieces of group work within a class; so allowing for the pupils' differing ability, their speed of progress, and classroom resources. The book is ideal for the 'roundabout' systems now used in many schools to give a 'taster' in all aspects of practical and creative work.

The subject of Home Economics is a wide and ever-changing one. We hope that this book will be valuable in helping pupils to use this important curriculum subject as a basis for healthy family life.

V. REYNOLDS
G. WALLIS
1987

Acknowledgements

The authors and publishers would like to thank the following for their help in the production of this book:

Peter Reynolds for compiling the index and further research
Peter Wallis for word processing and checking the script and
   both for their general help and support throughout

and for permission to reproduce photographs and previously published material:

The Controller of Her Majesty's Stationery Office (p. 38)
Gloucestershire Ambulance Service (p. 87)
Health Education Authority (p. 14)
Rex Features (p. 36)
Royal Society for the Prevention of Accidents (pp. 54, 77, 79
   and 86)
J. Sainsbury plc (pp. 122 and 123)
South Derbyshire Leisure Centre (p. 12)
The Sports Council (pp. 10 and 18)
Tesco Stores Ltd (pp. 122 and 124)

Family Life and Healthy Living

FAMILY LIFE

All families are different. A century ago the typical family consisted of:

Mum, Dad, children, Grandma and Grandad, all living together.

Aunty, Uncle, cousins, living close by.

This is called an **extended family** where at least three generations live together or nearby.

Circumstances were different from those found today:

- Dad went out to work and Mum stayed at home to look after the family and home.
- Families received little health care and financial aid.
- Housework was mainly manual and took a long time.
- Life expectancy was short and the infant mortality rate was high.
- Education was basic and finished at the age of 12 or 13.
- Diet was poor and the importance of healthy eating was not clearly understood.

1 Families of today often live in a **nuclear family.** Find out what this means.

2 Copy and complete this chart to show the reasons why families today have changed:

The family today	Reason(s)
Many mothers go out to work.	To help with the family income.
Employment prospects may require a family move.	
More leisure time is available.	
People are living longer.	
People are better educated and more independent.	
Food is more interesting and varied.	

Example (appears to the left of the first row)

Families differ because they contain a different mix of people. Examples are:

- A mother, father and one or more children.
- A one-parent family.
- A children's home.

Can you think of at least two other family situations and add them to the list?

One particular type of family is not better than any other – every family will succeed if everyone works together.

Choose the six cards which you consider most important in making a happy family.

Happy families

Scoring:

A–1 **B**–1 **C**–5 **D**–3 **E**–3 **F**–1 **G**–5 **H**–3 **I**–3
J–1 **K**–1 **L**–3 **M**–5 **N**–5

Add up your total score:

24–26 marks – you have chosen well.

16–23 marks – quite a good choice.

Under 16 marks – money and possessions are not that important.

HEALTHY LIVING FOR THE FAMILY

We should all be aiming for as good a standard of health as possible. Some people are lucky and do not become ill often; others are less fortunate but can still lead happy and interesting lives.

The chart below shows what is needed for healthy living.

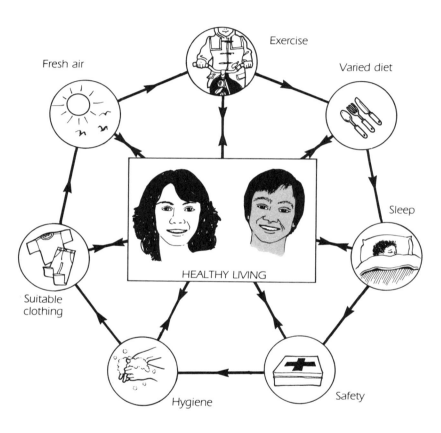

Make a list of the things which can *damage* your health, e.g. smoking.

Now let us look in detail at the requirements for healthy living.

Health and Body Maintenance

TAKING EXERCISE

To buy a new car we would have to pay several thousand pounds. We would clean and polish it, and inspect it regularly for any mechanical faults. It would be fed with petrol and oil, and several times a year it would have a thorough overhaul to check for safety and reliability.

Our bodies are much more complex than a motor car. We cannot throw away some parts and replace them with new ones, and yet many of us do not take as much care of ourselves as we would of an expensive motor car. Most of us neglect our bodies in some way. Some people abuse their bodies so badly with the use of drugs, alcohol and tobacco that irreparable damage is done.

Remember – good health and hygiene habits started in childhood should result in a healthier and fitter body for the adult. A badly maintained car will be unusable after a few years, but a well-looked after Rolls-Royce will last a very long time. In this section we will consider ways of establishing and maintaining bodily fitness.

The pictures on the previous page are examples of children at play. Which of these are they developing:

muscular skills	social skills
balance skills	precise movement
hand/eye co-ordination	vision, hearing, speech

They are not only developing their bodies but also helping their social and intellectual development.

What about adults?

As teenagers develop into adulthood, some may have the sort of jobs or be involved in activities where their body must be in the peak of condition:

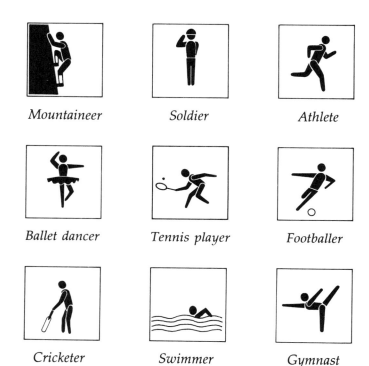

Mountaineer	Soldier	Athlete
Ballet dancer	Tennis player	Footballer
Cricketer	Swimmer	Gymnast

Which famous people do you know who are associated with any of these activities? Look for their pictures in newspapers and magazines and make a class poster.

These are the things that *they* do to maintain perfect health and control over their bodies:

Take
- exercise
- fresh air
- rest

Avoid	●	stress
	●	smoking, alcohol, drugs
Control	●	cleanliness
	●	diet (as you will see in the next section)
	●	mental attitudes.

Most people could not follow the same strict regime as the professional gymnast or any of the other people in these pictures. However, we can all follow their example in many ways during our leisure time.

WHAT – is exercise?

We all take exercise during our normal daily routine but sometimes we choose to develop an interest or hobby to maintain or reach a certain level of fitness. Many people sit at a desk all day and spend much of their leisure time in front of the television. It has been estimated that for every hour participating in sport we spend 75 hours just watching it.

Does this apply to you?

Exercise and achieving personal fitness need not be boring and over-strenuous. It can be:

- ● fun
- ● simple
- ● energetic
- ● relaxing
- ● interesting
- ● rewarding
- ● sociable
- ● adventurous
- ● intellectual.

WHY – do we need it?

The aims of physical fitness are:

- ● to keep our body in good health
- ● to help prevent illness.

Your body was designed to cope with physical activity.

Do you hate it or enjoy it?

You may not wish to be a superstar but do you really want to put your health at risk? Experts agree that exercise is physically beneficial and can also be psychologically helpful. We all need to 'let off steam' occasionally. Angry outbursts and arguments release negative feelings, but playing hard for your team can also help to change your feelings and moods.

1 Think of all the activities you do which involve exercise. Why do you do them? Some of the reasons are physical, some are emotional, and some are social.

Try to identify which is which.

Copy the chart and put a tick in one of the columns.

	Physical	Emotional	Social

- I want to be more active.

- I want to get better at my sport.

- I think I'm going to be a superstar.

- I have fun with my friends.

- I want to be less clumsy.

- It helps me to relax and enjoy myself sensibly.

- It develops my muscles.

- I feel fitter after exercise.

- It will keep my body healthier in later life.

- I want to look fit.

- I am forced to do it.

- It develops my mind.

You may be able to add other reasons.

A First Home Economics Course

2 In your books, write down three of your own activities which help your physical, emotional or social development. Complete a chart like this:

	My Activity	Why?
Example	Swimming	I like it because I feel more relaxed after a swimming session.

Ever thought of sport?

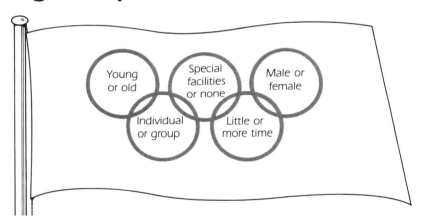

There is something to suit everyone. 'Sport for All' is a motto devised by the Sports Council to encourage everyone to be involved in any one of the hundreds of activities available.

Your school will give you a taste of several forms of sport and may even operate sporting achievement schemes. What do you think is the value of these schemes? You could ask your PE teacher more about them.

Try to find out some information about the history of the Olympic Games.

These are some of the reasons why athletes succeed. You may be able to add more. Try putting them in order of importance for the sport *you* enjoy the most:

Priority	Reasons why athletes succeed
	a determination to succeed
	b physical strength
	c courage
	d endurance
	e selfishness
	f competitive spirit

Sport in the community

The Sports Council is promoting a 10-year programme between 1983 and 1993 to encourage and help people to take up a sporting activity and to increase the opportunities available to play sport.

At the moment, less than half the population of Britain take part regularly in sport. Of those who do, the majority are men between the ages of 20 and 45. The aim of the Sports Council is to get 1.7 million more men and 3.9 million more women playing one or more sports by the end of the programme.

Included in these figures are two particular age groups who tend to drop out of sport at present:

the 13–24 year olds

the 45–59 year olds

To enable the Sports Council to fulfil its aims, money is being spent to increase the provision of:

- better community facilities
- a national indoor arena
- a national outdoor arena
- better coaching and administration for 20 selected sports
- national training centres for 11 different sports.

1 These people could all benefit from physical exercise.

a) A young couple, new to an area, both of whom are at work in the local town.

b) An enthusiastic 16-year-old starting on an apprenticeship scheme.

c) A mother at home all day with two pre-school children.

d) An 18-year-old with his or her own car, wishing to meet other people of a similar age and with similar interests.

e) A wheelchair-bound teenager wanting to develop a wider range of interests and meet new people.

f) An unemployed father of three with little prospect of obtaining a new job soon.

Choose at least three activities from the following list which could suit these people and explain your choice:

ice-skating	keep fit	hockey
walking	archery	horse-riding
running	fishing	tug-of-war
netball	gym	cycling
potholing	dancing	tennis
orienteering	judo	squash
canoeing	roller-skating	aerobics
football	green bowling	golf
jogging	yoga	sailing
badminton	swimming	
5-a-side football	athletics	

Where might they find information about their chosen activities?

2   Find out about the sports and competitions run by your nearest sports centre. Make a survey showing:

- how much each one costs
- how long you would be involved per session
- the age range covered.

3   Look for sports reports in your local or national newspaper.
Evaluate the information. What points do the reports cover? Write your own report of a recent sporting activity you have been involved in, covering similar points.

discussion area

What sports are offered:

a) in your local park?

b) at your local youth club?

Which of them have *you* made use of?

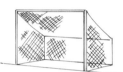

HOW – do we get fit?

The Health Education Authority offers sound advice to all age groups; ... 'the vital thing about getting fit is getting started'.

Here are some sensible precautions to consider before starting regular exercise:

- Consult your doctor if you have had problems such as high blood pressure, chest trouble, painful joints, a recent illness or operation, or are concerned about other health aspects.
- Be prepared to start slowly and build up a routine gradually.
- Find enough time to suit you and your chosen activity so that exercise is regular and not just in occasional bursts.

Regardless of age, sex or body shape, we can all achieve a better level of fitness by regular exercise.

Compared with a machine:

- the human body is only 16–27 per cent efficient,

however,

- the human body with regular exercise can be 56 per cent efficient.

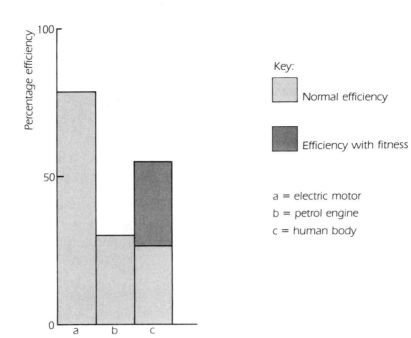

Graph to compare the percentage efficiency of the electric motor, petrol motor and human body

There are many different types of exercise. For general fitness it should involve every part of the body. The important things are to take regular exercise and to make sure that it is of the right type.

Regular exercise keeps:

The skeleton developing well

A good posture

Joints moving smoothly

Muscles in tone

Tendons supple

Our body shape in trim by using up calories/kilojoules

The heart, blood vessels and lungs working efficiently

Set a target of three periods of exercise per week each lasting 20 to 30 minutes.

The S factors

There are three factors which help towards general fitness:

S tamina

S uppleness

S trength

S tamina

This is staying power; the ability to keep going without gasping for breath. Exercises are designed to train your heart and lungs to make it possible for you to keep going for longer periods.

S uppleness

This is flexibility and mobility of muscles and joints. It keeps them in good working order. Some exercises designed for this are particularly useful for older people and those with arthritis.

S trength

Exercises tone up the muscles and enable them to take more strain.

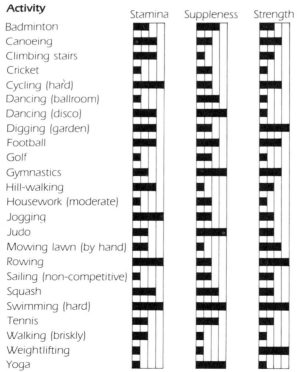

Activity

Badminton
Canoeing
Climbing stairs
Cricket
Cycling (hard)
Dancing (ballroom)
Dancing (disco)
Digging (garden)
Football
Golf
Gymnastics
Hill-walking
Housework (moderate)
Jogging
Judo
Mowing lawn (by hand)
Rowing
Sailing (non-competitive)
Squash
Swimming (hard)
Tennis
Walking (briskly)
Weightlifting
Yoga

Stamina   Suppleness   Strength

This chart compares different activities for stamina, suppleness and strength. A combination of some of the activities will help you to develop overall fitness.

Key:
Limited effect
Beneficial effect
Very good effect
Excellent effect

Courtesy of the Health Education Authority's 'Look After Yourself' Project

A First Home Economics Course

Many everyday activities, such as tidying your bedroom or cleaning your bike or the car, involve exercise but, because *we have to do them* they are not often counted as useful exertions. However, as well as exercising our body they give us a feeling of satisfaction and a sense of achievement.

Study the $\boxed{S}$ factor table.

In your notebook, list four leisure/sport activities and four everyday activities in the table. Compare the two groups for Stamina, Suppleness and Strength, and assess their value.

How fit are you?

Before starting any vigorous exercise, it is a good idea to test your level of fitness by checking your pulse rate at rest and again after exercise to prevent overexertion.

The heart pumps blood through blood vessels to all parts of the body. At certain places on our body we can actually feel the blood being pumped along, e.g. at the wrist, in the throat – at these points we can check our heart beat or pulse rate.

It is interesting to compare different resting heart beat rates:

mouse = 650 heart beats per minute

elephant = 25 heart beats per minute

baby = 130 heart beats per minute

Mr Average = 72–76 heart beats per minute
Ms Average = 75–80 heart beats per minute

average 12-year-old = 90 heart beats per minute.

The fitter you are the lower your normal pulse rate. During exercise the pulse rate will rise, depending upon how fit you are.

There is a maximum rate at which your heart should beat during exercise and it is related to your age. Work out your own maximum pulse rate by doing the following calculation:

195 − your age = maximum number of heart beats per minute; e.g. for a person who is 40 years old: 195 − 40 = 155 beats per minute. You should aim for a figure just under this – if it is too high, slow down!

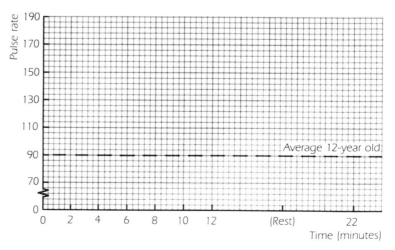

activity

1 Follow these instructions carefully to see if exercise does increase heart beat. Record the results accurately.

a) Sit comfortably and take your pulse. Place the first three fingers of one hand on the wrist of the other hand, about 2.5 to 5 cm away from the heel of the thumb.

b) Count the number of beats in 15 seconds and multiply by four to give the pulse rate per minute. Write down the result.

c) Now run on the spot for 2 minutes. Check your pulse again. Repeat this procedure six times, writing down the result each time.

d) Have a rest for 5 minutes and check your pulse.

e) Rest for a further 5 minutes and check your pulse again.

Your friend will time your activity and rest periods using a stop-watch or a clock with a second hand and write down the results each time.

Record your results in a graph like this:

A First Home Economics Course

2 What happened to your pulse rate
   a) at the end of the exercise session?
   b) after resting?

   Were you out of breath?

3 Compare your results with others in your group. What variations are there in resting pulse rates and activity pulse rates? Can you give reasons for any of these differences?

Starting an exercise programme

- Build up gradually then you will not give up.

- Make it a regular occurrence.

- Always do warm-up exercises.

- Be sensible in your choice of exercise and level of involvement.

- Choose exercises which you enjoy either alone or with others.

- Treat it like a hobby – perhaps your family can be involved.

- Choose an exercise to suit your pocket.

Be positive

It would be very easy to make excuses and never realise the benefits of being more active.

Read these two pieces carefully:

activity

A bloke I worked with down the market kept messing about, telling me I couldn't fight my way out of a paper bag. So I started working out down at the sports centre on the quiet. You should have seen his face last week when I picked up a sack of spuds in each arm. I saw <u>him</u> down at the sports centre last night.

It got pretty boring hanging around the local café in the evening after school. So when I saw this poster up about the roller disco, I thought I'd go down and have a look. It was fantastic. Plenty of music and laughs. Anyway, now I go skating two or three times a week. It's keeping me in shape and it's better than hanging around the café getting bored. I reckon you ought to get your skates on.

Now write endings for these stories:

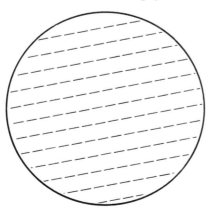

I bumped into an old mate down at the pub and I told him I was out of work and pretty bored. He plays for the local football team and said

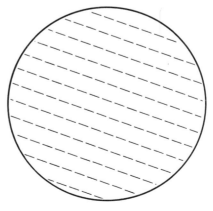

I was a bit quick on my feet at school. But I never really thought I'd keep it up after I'd left. Then this teacher said I should join

Make up your own situations:

discussion area

Discuss with your friends and family the types of exercise they prefer. Why do you think they enjoy them?

'We've formed a dance group at Youth Club. It's great fun. We're hoping to enter some competitions next year.'

'I go to a 50+ keep fit at the Church Hall. The people are very friendly and we always stay for a cup of tea and a chat afterwards.'

Exercise can be dangerous, especially if you are very unfit and do not have expert guidance.

Here are some useful **DO**s and **DON'T**s when you start taking more exercise:

DO

- wear something comfortable and suitable for your sport.
- eat a healthy balanced diet.
- some warm-up exercises to prepare your joints and muscles for action – it may help to prevent pulled muscles.
- some cooling down exercises which help to prevent muscle stiffness.
- set yourself a realistic target – your body is the best judge of what you can do.
- take a refreshing shower after exercise.
- learn all you can about your sport before you start and understand the safety procedures.
- get advice and tuition from an expert.

DON'T

- exercise too soon after a main meal – you may feel sick or get cramp.
- endanger your life or anyone else's just to prove a point. Think of other people's safety.
- attempt sudden and vigorous activity after a period of inactivity.
- push yourself 'till it hurts' – you may injure yourself or lose the enjoyment your sport should give you.
- exercise normally if you are recovering from an operation. Follow your doctor's advice.

DANGERS of exercise

By being careful and following the rules, most forms of exercise can be quite harmless. However, sometimes injuries occur, most commonly to:

- knees and ankle joints
- the head and neck
- tendons and muscles.

Often rest will overcome the problem but sometimes damage is severe and may need specialist treatment. Always take notice of any feelings of pain or strain before serious or even permanent damage is done.

Stitch or cramp pains are muscular reactions which can be caused by:

- over exercising – the muscles run short of the oxygen which helps them to work
- ignoring sensible precautions, e.g. swimming too soon after a meal.

Try resting for a short time if you have stitch. For cramp, although it is painful, stretch out the muscle and then massage it.

activity

1   Contact your local branch of the St John Ambulance Brigade or the British Red Cross Society and ask if someone may be able to talk to your group and give a demonstration of simple first aid treatment for sporting injuries.

A First Home Economics Course

2 List five common injuries which might occur during exercise and explain the action you would take. Fill in a chart like this:

Part of Body	Injury	Action
Ankle	Sprain	Cold water or ice, elastic support dressing, rest.

Example

FRESH AIR

Many of our activities whether as part of our daily routine or leisure time are done in the fresh air. This could be a reason why we enjoy doing that particular activity. Fresh air helps us to be:

- active
- alert
- healthy
- clear headed
- relaxed.

Fresh air may also give us a good appetite and can help us to sleep better.

Air which is not polluted by:

Fog or damp   Manufacturing waste   Petrol fumes   Smoke

will benefit our lungs and all our body cells whether we are at work, at play or asleep.

Air is made up of nitrogen, oxygen, and tiny amounts of a few other gases. In a dirty atmosphere the percentage of oxygen present will be reduced.

Nitrogen – is only breathed in and straight out again because it has no use in the body.

Oxygen – is needed for every cell in the body to work properly. We cannot live for more than 5 minutes without oxygen. Only approximately one-fifth of the oxygen in each breath is actually held in the lungs for transportation to the cells.

Carbon dioxide – is produced as a waste product in the cells and needs to be breathed out with each breath.

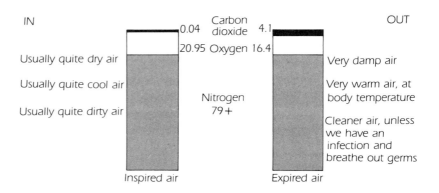

IN		OUT
	Carbon dioxide 0.04 → 4.1	
	Oxygen 20.95 → 16.4	
Usually quite dry air		Very damp air
Usually quite cool air		Very warm air, at body temperature
Usually quite dirty air	Nitrogen 79+	Cleaner air, unless we have an infection and breathe out germs
Inspired air		Expired air

The air we breathe

The air we breathe out is cleaner than the air we breathe in because the respiratory system filters out some of the impurities, such as dust.

Did you know that . . .

air pollution in industrialised countries such as ours is very dangerous? During the winter of 1952–3 the smoke mixed with the fog and the result was 'smog' which hung over the towns. In London 4000 people died from the effects of 'smog' which caused pneumonia and related chest infections. The Clean Air Acts of 1956 and 1968 have helped to control pollution in our cities and towns.

Being out in the fresh air may also mean we benefit from the action of sunlight on our skin:

- The ultraviolet rays react with a substance under the skin to form Vitamin D which is stored in the liver. Vitamin D is needed to produce strong bones and teeth.
- It has a healing effect on skin blemishes, e.g. spots.
- Some people like to tan their skin but too much sun in this way can cause headaches, sunburn and damage to the skin tissues.

A First Home Economics Course

Look at the list of activities on p. 11

a) How many of them are outdoor pursuits?

b) Make a list of everyday family activities which take place in the open air, e.g. taking the dog for a walk.

c) Look at your daily routine. Make a list of the ways in which you could get more fresh air and possibly more exercise, e.g. sleeping with your window open on pleasant evenings.

SLEEP

Although, scientifically, little is known about sleep, we do know the following:

- We can go for longer without food than we can without sleep.
- Sleep is vital for the health of our minds and to give our bodies 'time off' to rest.

Sleep patterns

Most body activities such as heart beat and breathing slow down during sleep. Our muscles relax and worn out cells are renewed. We aim to wake up feeling refreshed and mentally alert with renewed physical energy.

There are two kinds of sleep:

i) plain or deep sleep when the body, face and eyes are quiet and relaxed.

ii) Dream sleep when the body, face and eyes are active. This is called REM sleep because of the Rapid Eye Movements which scientists investigating sleep have noticed.

Both kinds of sleep are essential and each one happens in turn throughout the night, but it has been found that we especially need REM sleep.

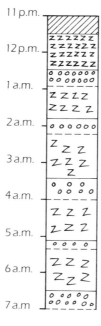

11 p.m.

12 p.m.

1 a.m.

2 a.m.

3 a.m.

4 a.m.

5 a.m.

6 a.m.

7 a.m

a) About 20 minutes to drift into a state of physical and mental inactivity.

b) The first phase is of plain sleep and lasts for about 1 hour.

c) The second phase is of dream (REM) sleep which lasts for several minutes.

Key:

z z z Plain sleep

° ° ° REM sleep

The sleep/dream phases b) and c) form a cycle which is repeated approximately five times during the night although the length of each phase may vary.

A typical night's sleep for an adult

Do you dream?

Everybody has dreams but we only remember them if we wake up during or immediately after the dream.

discussion area

- Do you remember your dreams?
- Do you sometimes dream about what you would like to be or do?
- Do your dreams ever come true?

Without giving away too many secrets, try to decide within your group if you think dreams are relevant and why some people attach a lot of importance to them.

Tossing and turning in your sleep should not affect the value of your sleep.

Did you know that . . .

we change body position between 25 and 40 times during an 8 hour period of sleep?

How much sleep should we have?

The recommended amount of sleep needed for different individuals varies according to their age, the type of work or amount of physical activity they do and the health of their mind or body. These are the average recommended amounts of sleep for:

Age	Length and type of sleep
Newborn baby	16–20 hours 50 per cent of this time is in plain sleep 50 per cent of this time is in dream sleep
2–3 years	About 11–12 hours 25 per cent of this time is in dream sleep
5–9 years	About 10–11 hours 20 per cent of this time is in dream sleep
14–18 years	About 10 hours 15 per cent of this time is in dream sleep
33–45 years	7 hours 20 minutes has been calculated as the average. Some people need more, others less, but generally the older we get, the less sleep we need. 25 per cent of this time is in dream sleep.

activity

1 Analyse the sleeping habits of members of *your family*. Put your answers in graph form to show:

a) the ages of the people
b) the hours they sleep.

How do they compare with the averages given above?

2 Now analyse *your own* sleeping habits in detail:
a) How well do you think you sleep?
b) Are you a restless sleeper?
c) When do you go to bed?
d) How much sleep do you think you need?
e) Do you sometimes wake in the middle of the night? Why do you wake up?
f) When do you need more sleep? Why?

Compare your comments with those of other people in your group.

Sleeping problems

As teenagers, there should be few occasions when you need to . . .

. . . but remember it is natural not to sleep well occasionally if you have a reason, e.g. a family problem or upset.

There are lots of things which could keep you awake such as:

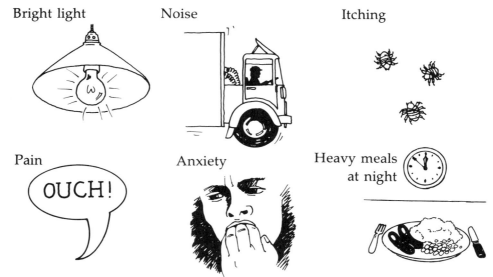

Bright light   Noise   Itching

Pain   Anxiety   Heavy meals at night

OUCH!

Insomnia means not being able to sleep. Some adults can suffer from this and one of the main causes is anxiety. They worry about not sleeping and then cannot sleep because they are worrying. It becomes a vicious circle! Prescribed sleeping drugs can help for a short time but they will not cure the cause of the anxiety. Missing a night or two of good sleep will probably make you 'on edge' or 'touchy' and more tired than usual. However, being deprived of sleep over a period of time will make your body and mind sluggish:

- You will not be able to react efficiently in an emergency.
- You cannot learn properly.

In extreme cases lack of sleep could contribute to mental breakdown.

Eight tips for a good night's sleep:

- Go to bed before you become over-tired.
- Try to relax before you go to sleep, e.g. read a few pages of a book, but don't try to do your homework.
- Take some exercise in the evening, e.g. walking, dancing.
- A warm bath and a warm drink can be soothing last thing at night.
- Set a regular bedtime for yourself.
- Make sure your bed is comfortable and your bedclothes are lightweight but warm enough.
- Leave a window open but make sure it is not draughty.
- Do not eat too much before going to bed.

Taking exercise, having fresh air and rest are all important factors in establishing and maintaining bodily fitness BUT this fitness can be easily destroyed if the body is abused. Therefore care should be taken to avoid . . .

STRESS

Everyone is different and each of us reacts differently to the everyday ups and downs in our lives. We need to try to understand the situations which lead us to worry.

Stress can be caused by:

- concern about other people's opinions of us
    - at home, at school, at work, at leisure
- pressures from society
    - the need to have a better life style – more money, a new car, expensive holidays
- pressures at work and at school
    - expecting us to do more than we can cope with
- particular situations
    - queueing at the supermarket checkout, failing an exam, noisy surroundings, sitting in a traffic jam, losing something important.

Stress is a normal part of life which only becomes a problem if it is allowed to build up. Remember the saying, 'Every cloud has a silver lining.' – we all have times when we feel low or a little depressed but we can soon cheer up and get on with everyday living.

However, too much stress, too often, can not only damage us physically, but also mentally, leading to severe depression which needs medical help.

These things could be signs of stress:

- always feeling tired in spite of having enough sleep
- suffering from niggling aches and pains without reason
- losing your temper quickly
- losing interest in yourself and others
- needing to eat, drink or smoke more than usual
- constantly feeling 'run down' with minor illnesses such as colds and headaches.

The body is designed to deal with stressful situations, e.g. waiting to go out on your first real date, playing in an important match, being at the scene of a road accident.

This is what happens:

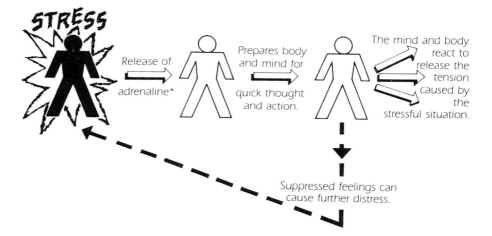

But *how* will you react? You could:

- bite someone's head off ● pick a fight ● shout and scream
- bite your nails ● cry ● be spiteful . . . and so on . . .

but it will not help you and it will not help other people.

Count to ten can be good advice as it gives us time to take a more positive line and think about our reactions. Try some of these simple ideas:

- breathe deeply – even count to ten
- talk to yourself in a calm, gentle way
- listen to soothing music to take your mind off the problem

*Adrenaline is the 'alarm' hormone which speeds up the pulse rate, increases blood pressure, causes muscles to tense, the body to sweat etc.

A First Home Economics Course

- walk away or go for a short walk for a few minutes
- be energetic, e.g. cycle to the shop for a magazine
- exercise regularly, e.g. do exercises each morning
- find an interesting hobby, e.g. fishing, sewing, sketching, computers
- tense your muscles then relax them in turn e.g. fingers, wrist.

Make a table like the one here and list some of the situations which might be stressful to you.

What would be your immediate reaction to them?

Now, stop and think.

In the last column, write down your reactions after sensibly considering the situation.

Here are a few suggestions to help you:

Situation	Immediate reaction	Stop and think
a) Your best friend teases you about your haircut in front of the class. You decide you have had enough.		
b) Your mum and dad will not let you stay out late. They are angry when you come home 2 hours late deliberately.		

To help you to understand your reactions and their effect on your body and health, list as many feelings as you can, e.g. truthful, happy, angry, loving, unkind.

Which do you think are negative feelings and which are positive?

Compare your list with other people's and discuss any differences there might be.

Making adjustments

It is not easy to adapt to a different life style but it is worth trying to do just that if it reduces the amount of stress we have to face. Some useful hints which you might like to consider working on are:

- learn to relax more to ease the tension away
- keep yourself fit and healthy
- make time for a hobby or interest – giving yourself a break from the pressures around you may help to take your mind off the problem
- face up to the feelings of stress and try not to be afraid of them – you cannot 'run away' for ever
- accept criticism – it may help you to understand yourself
- be helpful and friendly – sometimes others may need help too
- be optimistic about yourself – you really do have a lot of good in you.

BODY ABUSE

> - **WARNING: Smoking, Alcohol and Drugs can seriously damage YOUR HEALTH**

Yes, it *is* true. Tobacco, alcohol and drugs contain chemicals which can alter your body chemistry causing damage which, in some cases, can never be put right. Unfortunately, some people allow themselves to become dependent on these chemicals and let their habit of smoking too much, drinking too much or taking drugs which have not been prescribed, control them. People who choose to abuse their bodies in this way may also cause unhappiness to others, particularly their family and friends.

Initially, these body pollutants will give pleasurable sensations. Usually it is only when your health begins to suffer that you realise the long term damage that has been done.

Is it really worth it?

These are some of the more serious dangers to health associated with:

- smoking tobacco
- drinking alcohol
- taking drugs illegally.

Smoking tobacco

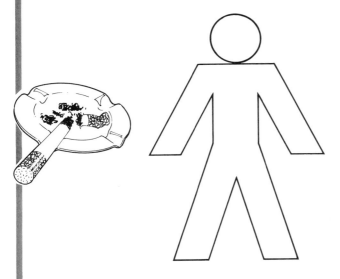

- Brain damage – strokes
- Frequent coughs and colds
- Cancers of the mouth, throat, larynx and lungs
- Chronic bronchitis and emphysema
- Heart attacks
- Stomach ulcers
- Cancers of oesophagus, pancreas, kidneys and bladder.

FACTS
- Smoking affects the unborn baby if the expectant mother is a smoker.
- Passive smoking, that is, breathing air polluted by tobacco smoke, can affect us all but especially children. It may even encourage children to start smoking.

Drinking alcohol

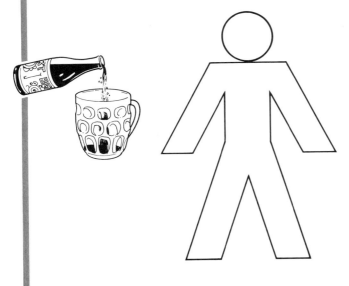

- Problems with the nervous system
- Brain damage
- Depression and other psychiatric disorders
- Cancers of the mouth, throat, oesophagus
- High blood pressure
- Stomach disorders – ulcers, gastritis
- Vitamin deficiencies
- Hepatitis
- Cirrhosis of the liver
- Sexual difficulties
- Problems for diabetics

- Drinking alcohol during pregnancy can damage the foetus.
- Drinking alcohol affects reactions to particular situations, self control and behaviour.

Taking illegal drugs

Drugs have been used for thousands of years and many of them, if used correctly, are useful and helpful in treatment of particular problems in the body. Some drugs are naturally present in drinks like coffee and cola, which contain caffeine, some may be bought over the counter, e.g. aspirin, and some are prescribed by a doctor, e.g. antibiotics. Unfortunately, a growing number of people, especially young people, are becoming addicted to illegal drugs. These drugs quickly take their effect physically and mentally.

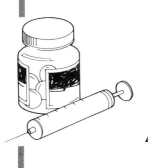
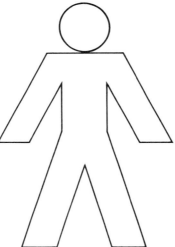

- Mental deterioration
- Many psychological hazards
- Breathing problems
- Damage to the nervous system
- Muscular spasms
- Damaged blood vessels and heart failure
- Skin abscesses
- Blood poisoning (if injected)
- Damage to liver and kidneys
- AIDS (from sharing infected needles)

FACTS

- If an expectant mother is a drug addict, her baby may also be one and may suffer serious withdrawal symptoms just after birth.
- The obsession for drugs can force drug addicts to steal and deceive to satisfy their needs.

Why do we

- smoke tobacco
- drink alcohol
- take drugs?

Consider each problem and assess why you think people start to smoke, drink alcohol, take drugs. What is your view about each habit? Fill in a table like the one below. Some examples are given.

Habit	Why do people do it?	I think that . . .
Smoking	a) It is sociable to smoke in company. b) . . .	Smoking is expensive . . .
Drinking	a) It gives me confidence. b) . . .	Hangovers are unpleasant . . .
Drugs	a) It is exciting to try something new. b) . . .	Prevention is better than cure . . .

Look at these facts:

- For every cigarette smoked you shorten your life by an estimated $5\frac{1}{2}$ minutes.

- Smoking the last 2 cm of a cigarette is more dangerous than the rest of the cigarette because the tar is more concentrated there.

- The risk of a smoker getting lung cancer is 25 times more than for a non-smoker.

- A smoker has bad breath, stained fingers and discoloured teeth. Hair and clothes smell.

- Smoking is expensive – just think what you could do with that sort of money.

- There are over eight million people in this country who have stopped smoking.

- On average, it takes 1 hour for the body to get rid of the alcohol in one standard drink.

- After drinking approximately 3 litres (6 pints) of beer at night, a person could still be over the legal limit to drive the next morning.

- A half-pint of beer has the same alcohol content as a single whisky (pub measures).

- People are more likely to have an accident at work or on the roads if they have drunk between 1 and 3 pints of beer.
- More than half the people breathalysed and convicted have more than twice the legal amount of alcohol in their blood.
- Road accidents after drinking are the biggest cause of death in young men.
- One in three of the drivers killed in road accidents are over the legal limit.
- Teenagers and women are generally more affected by alcohol than adult men because of their smaller body size.

- Alcohol with a sedative drug is a deadly combination.
- Overdoses of the 'hard' drugs are fatal.
- It is illegal to sell, possess or use drugs controlled under the Misuse of Drugs Act.
- The maximum prison sentence for one trafficking offence is 14 years.
- Caffeine, in drinks such as coffee and cola, can act as a mild stimulant if a lot is consumed.
- Hallucinating drugs totally confuse the mind and can lead to death.
- Accidents can easily happen whilst someone is affected by sniffing glue or solvents, e.g. falling into a canal or choking on vomit.

Perhaps you could research other interesting facts to add to these lists, e.g.: How much does it cost to smoke 20 cigarettes a day for a year? What is the legal limit of alcohol in the blood for a driver? What is alcoholism? What is a carcinogen? What is meant by a 'soft' drug? What does being an addict mean?

Young people often find that adolescence is a time for experimenting with new yet confusing feelings as they reach for maturity. The best advice to give to anyone is:

- Do not start smoking. If you *are* a smoker, stop now.

- It makes sense to drink sensibly for your own and others' health and safety.

- Just say NO. This could give you pleasurable feelings knowing that you are in control of yourself.

1   Divide into groups in your class and investigate ways in which people could change their smoking and drinking habits. Some examples are given below.

Smoking
• Save the money which would have been spent on cigarettes and give yourself a treat.
• Decide to become a non-smoker instead of a smoker. Know why you are making this decision and stick to it.
• Keep yourself busy when you would normally smoke.

Drinking
• Be aware of when, why, how much and with whom you drink.
• Go out with your friends later and try buying your own drinks – others may follow your idea.
• Only drink soft drinks before a meal if you are going to drink alcohol with it.

2   Read all about it! Look at the newspapers for headlines which illustrate the misuse of drugs or the abuse of alcohol. Make a classroom display and discuss your findings.

Drug addicts resort to hiding in a yard for their 'fix'

Does this picture make you stop and think?

Design a poster which would make a teenager stop and think seriously if they were tempted to begin a dangerous drug habit.

discussion area

a) Many companies advertise their brand of cigarette or drinks. Look at some examples from magazines. What effects do the advertisers hope to have on the consumer? Do you think that people are influenced by what they see and read in these advertisements? Are you?

b) What is your opinion about the effect on the viewing public of the sponsorship some of these companies offer to sporting events, e.g. cricket, snooker, motor racing?

Help is at hand

You must not give up trying to get yourself back on the road to healthy living.

Make a decision today – say NO! It is not easy but remember – it is *your* choice.

Do not leave it too long before seeking help.

Do not be afraid to ask for help.

Many people, including your family, friends, teachers, social worker or doctor will want to help you and give you their support if you discuss your problem with them. Several organisations offer counselling, advice and information. Here are some of them:

General enquiries

Health Education Authority
78 New Oxford Street
London WC1A 1AH
01 631 0930

Smoking

Action on Smoking and
Health (ASH) Ltd.
5–11 Mortimer Street
London W1N 7RH
01 637 9843

Alcoholism

Alcoholics Anonymous
PO Box 514
11 Redcliffe Gardens
London SW10 9BQ
01 352 9779

For relatives of alcoholics:
Al-Anon Family Groups
61 Great Dover Street
London SE1 4YF
01 403 0888

The Accept Clinic
200 Seagrave Road
London SW6
01 381 3155

Alcohol Concern
305 Grays Inn Road
London WC1X 8QF
01 833 3471

Drugs

Freefone 'Drug Problems' – dial 100 and ask for:

SCODA
1–4 Hatton Place
London EC1N 8ND
01 430 2341

Families Anonymous
88 Caledonian Road
London N1
01 278 8805

Drug abuse centres in your area.

Look at the case histories over the page as published by the DHSS.
Perhaps it is hard to see yourself in situations such as these but thinking that 'it won't happen to me' is a very dangerous attitude to take.

Helen, 16, disappointed Yorkshire girl

Going over the top can make small problems bigger

When Helen broke with her current boyfriend, nobody thought much of it. It seemed a normal part of teenage life. But Helen was depressed and upset. She knew that when her mother felt that way she took tranquillisers – a drug legally prescribed by the family doctor. So Helen tried it too, and it made her feel better. It wasn't long before her mother noticed that the tranquillisers were disappearing and when she found a capsule in Helen's bedroom, she put two and two together.

Angry and frightened, she immediately told Helen's father. They confronted Helen together and a fierce argument followed. This ended with Helen slamming tearfully out of the house and the tranquillisers being put under lock and key. This might have made sense earlier, but it was now too late to solve anything. The following week a schoolfriend gave Helen what was probably heroin, although neither of them were really sure. Nevertheless, it seemed exciting and sophisticated and – better still – it was a way of getting back at her parents.

Later still, she took up with a new boyfriend, older than herself and a regular drug user. Helen's parents were unaware of their daughter's deeper involvement in the drug scene until they heard about the new boyfriend being arrested for a drug offence. Realising they were out of their depth, they decided to seek help from a family guidance counsellor. He pointed out to them that they had over-reacted to the original tranquilliser incident, when it would have been better to deal calmly and understandingly with Helen's temporary romantic upset. Their better understanding of the way their daughter feels is now helping them to help her come to terms with life without drugs.

Mike, pupil at a Midlands comprehensive

Teachers and parents link to fight drug problem

One evening, Mike told his father that a classmate had been caught smoking cannabis at school. Mike himself had been offered a joint once or twice, but had turned it down. Although relieved at his good sense, Mike's parents were still worried that drugs seemed to be available at his school. They spoke to his form teacher and found out that it was a subject of concern for other parents, as well as the teaching staff. Shortly afterwards the PTA arranged an evening meeting, and it was agreed that drugs should be included along with other subjects covered in health education classes.

Talks for parents were arranged at the same time. This helped parents understand a subject they often felt they knew less about than their children. Both courses of action helped. Although the drug problem did not disappear, it became more manageable. Parents, teachers and children are now all better equipped to prevent a worrying situation getting out of control.

PERSONAL CLEANLINESS

Having taken the positive steps of trying to establish healthy routines and avoiding excess of stress and body pollutants, we should also try to maintain bodily fitness by controlling such things as cleanliness, diet and mental attitudes.

Personal cleanliness is a very important aspect of health care. Bodies which are being neglected soon begin to show the tell-tale signs of a lack of personal hygiene. These include:

- skin with ingrained dirt, especially on neck and ears and between fingers and toes
- skin rashes, sores, boils, bites etc., which have been scratched and neglected
- dirty, untrimmed finger- and toe-nails
- offensive body odour and bad breath
- greasy, unwashed, lank hair
- bad teeth, covered with plaque and stains
- a poor posture and personal appearance – because people who neglect their own cleanliness do not usually bother about their appearance.

Most of these conditions come about after a long period of neglect and can lead to serious ill-health. We can expect some of these conditions to occur quite naturally in some circumstances, e.g.:

Dirty skin and nails – after gardening or cleaning jobs.

Strong body odour – after prolonged exercise or as a natural result of menstruation or illness.

Skin rashes   – caused by allergies.

Bad breath   – caused by digestive disorders or gum and teeth infections.

Hair and nails in poor condition   – due to poor diet or illness.

Bad posture   – from over-tiredness or medical conditions such as asthma.

We are therefore looking at real cases of neglect rather than these occasional occurrences, most of which can be easily corrected.

The following chart shows some of the problems brought about by not looking after yourself, and gives examples of the possible causes.

In your notebook, suggest other possible causes and how to deal with the problem. Sometimes the only answer is a visit to the doctor, dentist or chiropodist because the condition is so badly neglected.

Problem	Possible Causes
Ingrained dirt in skin	Poor hygiene training
Cracked, dry skin	Use of cheap soaps and cosmetics
Greasy, spotty skin	Leaving stale perspiration and make-up on the skin
Skin rashes	Allergy to biological soap powders, certain foods and prescribed drugs
Cracked and split nails	Vitamin and mineral deficiency
Offensive body odour	Insufficient and inadequate washing
Bad breath	Neglected teeth and gums
Hair in poor condition	Inefficient washing and rinsing
Discoloured teeth	Lack of regular cleaning, leaving a layer of plaque on the teeth
Poor posture	Lack of confidence in your appearance.

Personal profile

CARE

Hair
Do you wash your hair
regularly, use a good
quality shampoo and
keep your brush and
comb clean?

Eyes
Do you wear your glasses
as prescribed and avoid
watching too much TV?

Ears
Do you clean inside and
behind your ears carefully?
Do you change and
clean earrings regularly?

Teeth
Have you got a regular
dental routine, visit your
dentist, and avoid sugary
food and drink?

Skin
Do you bathe regularly,
shower after exercise, use
mild soaps and skin
products, and avoid
picking spots?

Odour
Do you smell clean and
fresh and change under-
clothing regularly?

Hands and **Nails**
Do you wash and dry
your hands well and use
handcream if they get
chapped? Do you brush
your nails and manicure
them regularly, eating
plenty of calcium foods?

Feet
Do you wash them
thoroughly and check for
athlete's foot and
verrucas? Do you choose
your footwear carefully?

PRESENT CONDITION

Is your hair clean, well
brushed and manageable?

Can you see clearly? Are
your eyes clear, bright
and well rested?

Are your ears clean and
hearing good?

Are your teeth strong and
regular, well brushed and
without cavities?

Is your skin firm, free from
spots and pimples, fresh
and clean?

Is your clothing clean and
fresh and do you smell
pleasant?

Are your hands and nails
clean? Are the nails well
manicured? Do you
protect your hands and
nails when doing dirty or
heavy work?

Can you walk and run
comfortably? Are your
socks and shoes
comfortable? Are your
feet clean and odour
free?

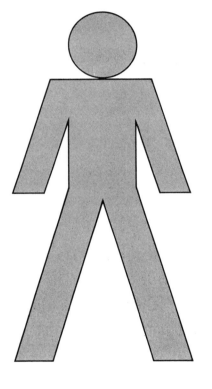

Do you have a positive attitude towards personal hygiene
and freshness and follow a daily hygiene routine?

How do you rate in the 'self maintenance' stakes? Try this
personal appraisal test. Be honest with the scoring, remember
we all neglect ourselves at times.

Personal score

Copy this chart. In column A give yourself a mark out of five for the present condition of your hair, eyes etc. In column B give yourself a mark out of five for the amount of care you give to that part of your body.

Part of the body	A Present condition	B Amount of care given
Hair Eyes Ears Teeth and gums Skin Hands and nails Feet and nails Posture Positive attitude to hygiene		

Scoring

A Present condition   45–30 ☺ very good

29–18 😐 a good try

17–1 ☹ more effort needed

B Care given – score as above. Add your two scores together.

The higher your marks – the nicer you are to know!

Here is a list of sensible DO's and DON'T's to remember when considering personal cleanliness – you may be able to think of some more.

DO

establish a simple cleanliness routine.

seek help if minor problems do not respond to simple remedies.

use good-quality products.

WHY?

It will become automatic and part of your lifestyle.

They probably need expert medical attention.

Cheap soaps and toiletries can damage the skin, hair and nails.   *continued*

read instructions on the package carefully.	To make sure that it will suit your skin, hair, nails, etc.
give any treatment you are trying time to work.	Some conditions such as athlete's foot or acne take several weeks to improve.
keep all equipment such as flannels, toothbrushes etc, clean and replace frequently.	Old equipment can cause or renew infections.
think about your diet, state of health and emotional condition.	They can all contribute to hygiene problems.

DON'T

WHY?

think that strong perfume will cover body odour.	It only makes it worse.
put clean clothes on a dirty body.	It does not make sense.
use antiperspirants to excess.	The body needs to perspire.
panic if you find evidence of fleas, nits or other parasites.	They can easily be got rid of (see later in this section).
ignore your problem hoping it will go away.	It usually gets worse if neglected.
be embarrassed about seeking help.	Everyone has similar problems. Your friends, your parents, the school nurse, teachers, chemists, and doctors will advise you.
use a medical preparation, e.g. skin cream, prescribed for someone else.	It could harm you.
become obsessed by cleanliness.	Our bodies are built to resist normal amounts of bacteria; excessive concern can lead to phobias.
be very influenced by TV or magazine advertising.	Manufacturers are out to sell their products, but you must make a sensible assessment of them and avoid impulse buying.

Below is a selection of advertisements for well-known hygiene and beauty preparations. Prepare a **fact file** of similar products and conduct a consumer survey to find out which products do their jobs well and which are good value for money.

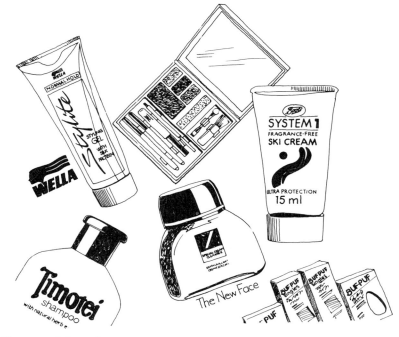

Commercial products

How to conduct the consumer survey:

i) Within your class, divide into five groups. Each group will study a selection of products which are advertised for care and treatment of the skin, the hair, the teeth, the nails or the feet.

ii) Each member of the group will test a different product.

iii) You can ask your family and friends if they have used the product and what they think of it.

Having researched the product you should then be able to make an informed assessment and evaluate its effectiveness. You could ask these and similar questions:

- Is the product expensive?

- Are you paying a lot for packaging and advertising?

- Is it very highly coloured and scented?

- After you had tried the product for several days or several times, did you notice an improvement, i.e. was the treatment a success or a failure?

- Could the product cause unpleasant reactions or side effects such as allergies, skin problems, hair loss etc.?

44

- Is it a reliable brand name which has been well tested?

- Does the package give clear instructions?

- Is it simple to use?

- Could you buy another brand which is cheaper, simpler and does the job as well or better?

- Why did you buy it? Were you attracted by the advertising, the appearance, the packaging, the colour and perfume, because someone recommended it?

Finally, you should be able to report:

- It is good/poor value for money.

- I would/would not recommend it.

It is easy to be hygienic if:

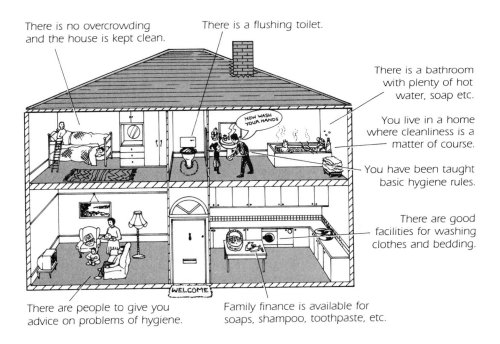

There is no overcrowding and the house is kept clean.

There is a flushing toilet.

There is a bathroom with plenty of hot water, soap etc.

NOW WASH YOUR HANDS

You live in a home where cleanliness is a matter of course.

You have been taught basic hygiene rules.

There are good facilities for washing clothes and bedding.

There are people to give you advice on problems of hygiene.

Family finance is available for soaps, shampoo, toothpaste, etc.

WELCOME

discussion area

What are the important points of hygiene which should be taught to children as soon as they are old enough to understand their meaning?

Draw up a 'Ten Point Plan' for a family to follow, which could include:

- Always clean your teeth after meals and use your own toothbrush.

- Always wash your hands after going to the toilet and before meals.

- Always leave the bathroom clean and tidy for the next person to use.

Finish the list with the points which you consider important.

It is not so easy to be hygienic if:

you live in a poor *environment* where
- inadequate washing facilities and lack of privacy may make it difficult to keep clean.
- lack of hot water and unheated rooms make washing cold and uncomfortable.
- the sink, bathroom, or toilet, have to be shared by a lot of people.
- conditions are dirty and overcrowded, so encouraging infestations of vermin and parasites.
- families are not educated in the ways of being hygienic and the reasons for personal cleanliness.

These are severe problems but they can be overcome if *you* have the will to do so. Even if no one else bothers about your personal freshness, your own self respect should make you do your best.

It was only during the last century that scientists began to think that there could be a connection between dirt and disease. Researchers discovered that we share our world with millions of different types of bacteria.

FACTS
- Bacteria are microscopic, one-celled organisms which live in or on the body and in the atmosphere surrounding us.
- They need food, warmth and moisture to survive and multiply; some also need oxygen.
- Some bacteria are harmless.
- Some can cause illness. They can enter the body through the natural openings to produce food poisoning, and infections such as whooping-cough, diphtheria and sore throats.

- The skin encases the body and protects it. An open, neglected wound allows bacteria to penetrate and set up infection.

**a moist, warm, dirty skin
with an open wound   = infection and disease
+ disease bacteria**

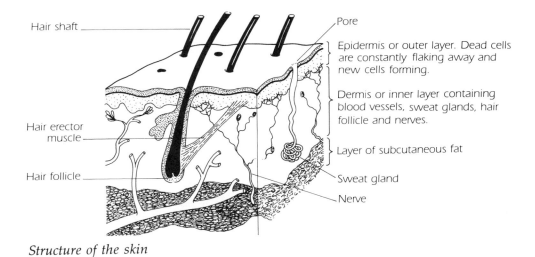

Structure of the skin

The skin cannot do its work efficiently if the pores are blocked with grease and dirt, or wounds and spots are neglected and dirty.

Infections and disease can also be spread by the **parasites** which live in or feed from the human body. The main ones are:

- fleas
- lice
- bedbugs
- mites

these are all parasites with very strong jaws used to pierce the skin of animals and humans and suck blood.

Human flea

Fleas – have strong claws for clinging on and powerful long back legs for jumping. As well as the human flea, there are fleas which usually live on animals such as cats, dogs and rats, but they will also attack humans. Flea bites become swollen and inflamed and if scratched can cause infection. Rat flea bites are especially dangerous.

Body louse

Body lice – are of three types; those which live on the body, those which live on the head, and those which live in the pubic hair (crab lice). They have strong claws to hold on with and their bite causes irritation. If scratched the wound can become infected and cause disease. *Head lice* lay their sticky eggs on the hair shaft and are fairly easy to detect.

Head louse   *Head louse nit*

Bedbugs – usually hide in crevices during the day and feed at night. The bite can be very irritating but it does not usually cause disease.

Mites – bites from these cause scabies which appears as groups of scabbed pimples on the body. They are very contagious and need immediate treatment.

Mite

Bedbug

All these parasites are very unpleasant and we usually panic if we realise that we have become infested. It is important to remember:

- Parasites can easily be transmitted from person to person or from other people's garments or belongings, seats in public transport etc.

- They will not just go away if they are ignored. They usually multiply very quickly, so they must be dealt with at the first signs.

- A few bites are not usually dangerous and will not spread disease, unless they are scratched and become infected.

- There are many powerful insecticides and antiseptics to deal with them and they are quite easily treated. A chemist, nurse or doctor will give advice.

- If one member of a family becomes infested, others in the family should check to see that they are not.

- Once the parasites have been dealt with, all the clothing, bed linen, flannels, hair brushes and combs etc., should be thoroughly cleaned.

- Fleas and bedbugs lay their eggs in floorboard cracks, carpets, beds and on pets, so these will all need thorough cleaning after infestation. Insecticide dust should be applied in the home and pets sprayed or dusted with insecticide.

If *you* discover you have:

flea bites – try to find the culprit and squash it. Wash and thoroughly clean all your clothing and bedding. Tell the people you live with so that the home and any pets can be treated with insecticide if necessary.

scabies – report the infection to your parents, or school nurse or doctor. It is very contagious and needs treatment.

head lice – go to the chemist for a special lotion called Prioderm or a similar strongly medicated shampoo. Continue using this until the lice are dead. Comb the hair with a fine-toothed comb to remove the remaining lice and nits. Avoid getting in close contact with other people and wash all pillowcases, scarves, hats, brushes and combs, and anything else which comes into contact with the hair.

Parasitic worms – live in the intestines of humans. The worms or their eggs can be picked up from animals and animal faeces, or may be passed into the body from infected food.

Threadworms

Threadworms – are about 5 mm ($\frac{1}{4}$ in) long and look like tiny pieces of white cotton. They are quite commonly found in children who have played in dirty conditions. They cause itching and tummy upsets. A doctor will give treatment and the whole family must be treated as threadworms spread very easily.

Roundworm

Roundworms – are up to 10 cm (4 in) long and live in the intestines and other organs. They are usually spread by infected food.

Tapeworm

Tapeworms – grow within the intestine. They can grow very long, small pieces breaking off and being passed in the faeces. Severe infection and debility can develop. Tapeworms are usually introduced into the body with undercooked meats and fish. They can be treated and eliminated with drugs.

Many of these infestations can be very easily picked up through contact with infected people or articles. However, normal standards of personal cleanliness and hygiene in the home will reduce the risks of serious results, and the parasites can be eliminated quickly and efficiently.

As we have seen, there are two main reasons for maintaining a high standard of personal cleanliness:

● So that we feel clean, fresh and attractive – this helps to boost our self confidence and makes us nice to be with.
● To reduce the risks of infection and disease which can be spread when our bodies are neglected.

It is easier for some people to be personally clean than it is for others because of their circumstances, but everyone can try hard – the end results are a good reward for all the effort.

discussion area

Discuss the following situations within your group. Decide the circumstances which may have caused them. Try to suggest some course of action which could help.

Jane and Tom are both 12 years old. They live at home with their parents in healthy surroundings with an adequate family income. Their parents give them quite a lot of pocket money and expensive presents.

Situation 1

JANE

Jane is overweight, always tired, usually miserable, has a spotty skin, greasy hair, does not smell pleasantly and is generally unattractive. No wonder she is unhappy; no one really wants to be near her, although she is kind and generous and would love to be one of the group.

How would you help her?

Write a *maintenance plan* for Jane using some of these points to help you:

● a medical check to make sure that there are no serious problems ● diet ● exercise ● sleep and rest ● cleanliness ● attitude to work ● parental influence ● mental attitude ● her character ● clothing.

Decide

a) the things she should put into action immediately, such as a personal hygiene routine and

b) the things she should introduce gradually, such as starting exercise.

A First Home Economics Course

TOM

Tom is pale and listless, very tall and thin, and has a poor appetite. He wears spectacles and is considered a bit of a swot. He does not like exercise as it makes him feel even more tired and he usually spends most of his time indoors watching TV or reading.

Do a *maintenance plan* for Tom, considering some of the points suggested in Jane's list.

Decide which of these things could be causing his general lack of good health:

● lack of exercise ● poor diet ● insufficient fresh air ● too much study ● worrying about his work ● lack of outside interests ● lack of confidence ● insecurity.

How could Tom be helped
a) straight away?
b) gradually?

Situation 2

Your friend is becoming very careless about her appearance, her hair looks dull and untidy, you notice a 'tide mark' round her neck and her breath is offensive.

Discuss the possible reasons.

Suggest the course of action you could take remembering that you would need to be very tactful!

Situation 3

Your teenage brother has an unpleasant pimply rash on his face. You know he is self-conscious about it and you would like to help. Discuss the possible reasons for the condition.

Suggest a course of action to help your brother but which would not offend him.

MENTAL ATTITUDES

Much of what we have learnt so far has been to do with factors which help or hinder our body maintenance, but closely linked with physical well-being are our emotional and mental attitudes. Some people are fortunate in possessing very healthy bodies and yet they are always grumbling and feeling sorry for themselves – they present a very poor image of themselves. Others are born with or develop some physical or mental handicap which may make every day a struggle for them and yet they always try to appear cheerful and make the most of the strengths which they possess.

Life would be very dull if things always ran smoothly and free from problems. It is our nature to strive and reach out for higher goals – that is how we have conquered Everest, reached the moon and have beaten many diseases, but to achieve these goals we must also be prepared to accept defeat and keep trying.

Adolescence is an 'in between' stage and everyone goes through this period, but for everyone the process is different. The normal teenager alternates between being a child and being an adult. The body is going through many physical and emotional changes and moods swing violently from high to low.

Pressures are exerted from outside influences such as TV, radio and cult figures and these may conflict with authority, such as your family, school and community.

However, the teenage years are an exciting time as new experiences unfold and you begin to plan your own future.

YOU:
see examples of good and bad actions all around you
set your own standards
choose which example to follow.

To be an achiever you need these qualities:

- a sense of humour – can you laugh at yourself as well as at others?
- perseverence – to keep trying even after several defeats
- a thirst for knowledge – there is always plenty to learn
- a spirit of adventure – always being ready to try to do something worthwhile
- the will to succeed
- honesty with yourself – recognise your good qualities and try to improve the poor ones
- confidence in yourself – to be able to accomplish what you set out to do.

All of these things are attitudes of mind – how many of them do you possess?

These guidelines should help you to have a healthy mind as well as a healthy body:

- You should like yourself, other people will accept you as you present yourself.

- Have a secure foundation to work from such as a group of friends, involvement in local community activities, a firm family commitment, a Youth Club or religious beliefs.
- Aim for good relationships with others by your loyalty and willingness to help.
- Let people know that you care – keeping in touch with family and friends is important.
- Accept criticism and learn from it.
- Don't be a 'ditherer' – learn to make decisions and stick to them.

Emotional upsets are part of life but there will always be times when we feel that we cannot cope and we need help with our problems. These people can help:

- your parents
- your teacher
- your doctor or community nurse
- a professional counsellor
- your friends
- a religious adviser
- a youth leader
- a magazine problem page.

'A problem shared is a problem halved.' Just talking to someone else about a situation can often help you to sort things out.

Perhaps you can help to solve some of your difficulties by helping others who are even less fortunate than you are. The sick, the handicapped, the elderly, the voluntary societies are always in need of a helping hand. Next time you feel bored or lonely, could you spend some time helping an elderly neighbour with the shopping or baby-sitting for a harassed mother?

During childhood you are allowed to learn from your mistakes, put failure behind you and make fresh starts. Part of growing up is learning how to stand on **your** own two feet and be responsible for **yourself** and for others.

Making the right choices will promote physical and emotional well-being.

Section Two

Health and Safety

ACCIDENTS IN THE HOME

To be SAFE means to feel secure and to be free from danger or risks.

Every year in the UK there are:
    15 000 accidental deaths (includes 1000 children)
    1 million injuries (includes 140 000 children).

- You have a 1 in 40 chance of being killed or injured in a home accident this year.
- Accidents account for about 30 per cent of all deaths in childhood (1–14 years).

At home we should feel secure BUT there are more accidents likely to happen in or around the home than anywhere else. These figures show that we are not secure; not free from danger.

Accidental deaths in homes and residential institutions (UK – 1983)

Ages	0–4	5–14	15–44	45–64	65+	All ages	Non-fatal*
Falls	26	1	114	302	3020	3463	$\frac{1}{2}$ million
Poisoning	4	8	276	153	110	551	20 000
Scalds flames and fire	77	41	105	145	435	803	70 000
Choking and suffocation	57	20	126	106	160	469	13 000
Other causes	41	9	76	80	229	435	350 000
Totals	205	79	697	786	3954	5721	953 000

*(only approximate figures are available)

These figures were compiled by RoSPA which is the Royal Society for the Prevention of Accidents (further information on p. 88).

Study the information in the chart on p. 54, then answer these questions.

a) Which age group is the most at risk of accidental death?

b) Suggest some reasons for this.

c) Which is the most common type of accident?

d) Why do you think this may be so?

e) Which age group is most at risk from fire?

f) Suggest some types of accidents which could come under 'other causes'.

g) What is the main cause of accidental death for 0–14 year olds?

Accidents in the home can happen to anyone, but the people most at risk are:

- young children who do not understand the dangers involved
- elderly people who may be unsteady on their feet, are hard of hearing, have failing eyesight or are generally not well
- those with physical or mental handicap
- the expectant mother who may be less agile or less steady than usual.

CAUSES AND PREVENTION OF ACCIDENTS

Make an accident survey amongst your friends. Try to get information about all age groups and the different types of accidents. You will need to ask at least five people in each age group which types of accidents they have had over the last 12 months. When you assess your information you should be able to state:

a) The age group which is most at risk.

b) The commonest type of accident.

c) The severity of damage most likely to occur.

Your chart should look like this (but with the different shaded areas varying in size):

	0-12 years	Teens	20 and over	Elderly
Falls				
Poisoning				
Scalds and burns				
Choking and suffoca-tion				
Cuts and grazes				
Road accident				
"Near miss"				

KEY [////] Serious injury involving going to hospital   [\\\\] Less serious injury   [ ] Minor injury

Most accidents need not happen.

They are caused by carelessness and lack of foresight. These are some other factors which can cause accidents:

To children

lack of parental training or guidance

lack of adult supervision

impulsive actions

children under stress

To adults

bravado and 'showing off', especially amongst young men

insufficient safety training at work

uncontrollable feelings e.g. anger, jealousy, impatience

use of drugs or alcohol

continued

negligence and carelessness of others	irresponsible behaviour with no thought for others
the small stature of children makes them difficult to see	carelessness when using tools and equipment
lack of physical strength	being under stress e.g. a quarrel at home or pressure of work
a sense of adventure and daring	
showing off to friends	tiredness or other physical weakness
bad behaviour and 'mucking about'	

Some of these factors are physical and some are emotional. Can you identify which are which?

We can help to keep ourselves safe by:

- being safety conscious at all times
- showing consideration for others
- avoiding dangerous situations
- using safety equipment
- choosing the correct equipment for its purpose
- keeping things in good repair
- not taking silly risks.

There are some things over which we have no control. Environmental factors such as weather, land slides and floods cause many accidents. All we can do is to listen to the warnings and take sensible precautions, e.g. wear protective clothing, keep away from trees in a storm, stay indoors if possible in bad weather conditions.

1 Try to be aware of potentially dangerous situations. Copy this list into your book.

All of these things could cause an accident. How many of them have you got in your home? Put a cross against them in the column and try to do something about it.

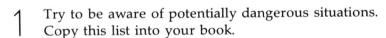

A worn rug or carpets – especially on the stairs.

No safety gate for the stairs if there is a baby in the family.

Poor lighting on the landing.

Electrical equipment with frayed wires or cables.

continued

Cleaning fluids kept at floor level within reach of children.

Old medicines and tablets still stored in the medicine cabinet.

A chair or table with a 'rickety' leg.

Matches left lying about.

Rugs put over polished floors.

Add any other dangers to this list.

2 In the panel below there are a number of different types of accident. Match them to the different danger situations in the pictures.

> falls   drowning   burns   scalds   electric shock
> poisoning   suffocation

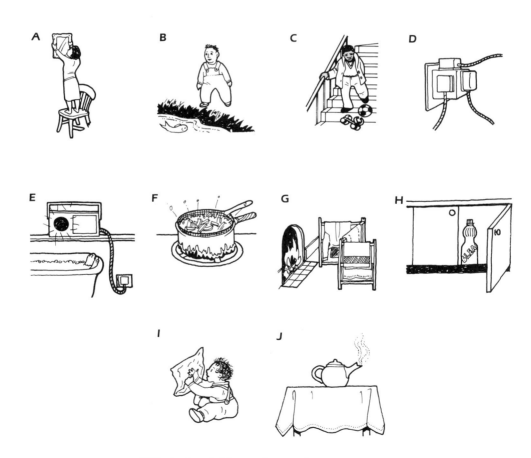

What should have been done to avoid each of these dangers?

3 Prevention is better than cure and if we use our common sense most accidents can be avoided. There are lots of safety 'gadgets' to help us. These pictures show some of them. Write a sentence about each one, explaining its purpose and the age group which would find it most useful.

Dummy plug

Safety gate

Cooker guard

Cupboard lock

Bed barrier

Bottle tongs

Lead-free paint

Round-ended scissors

Safety harness

Bottle with safety cap

Non-slip bath mat

Step stool

Safety film stuck on glass door

Corner cushions for table corners

Safety equipment

Manufacturers of goods and equipment used in the home should be safety conscious. To help them to produce consistently safe goods the British Standards Institute (BSI) provide guidelines and tests. Companies may choose to comply with the standards set by the BSI, and their products are then given a BS number and can carry a Kitemark or Safety Mark:

BS 857

Kitemark

Safety Mark

The consumer can then have confidence in the product and may be encouraged to buy it.

For some products, e.g. cots, car safety restraints for children, crash helmets and prams, manufacturers must follow BSI guidelines by a government regulation. Many manufacturers have brought out their own safety codes. Electrical, gas and oil appliances are all produced to rigid safety standards. They have their own labels which indicate to customers that the product has been thoroughly tested.

1   Look for these labels on goods in your own home or at school. Make a list of the ones you can find and explain how they help to keep us safe.

BEAB Approved

OAMA Mark

Safety signs and labels

2 Many houses have a garden and the garden can be just as hazardous as the house. The picture below shows some situations which could be dangerous.

See how many you can find and describe the accidents which could occur. How could these accidents have been avoided?

Hazards such as broken glass, garden ponds, gates left open, weed killer, etc. are obvious, some dangers are not so clear:

- **insect poisons and plant sprays:** gardeners often use commercial products, such as slug bait, to poison pests, and they spray plants and trees with chemicals. If picked up and eaten by children or animals, the effects can be especially severe.

- **garden toys** which are left outside all the time can become dangerous. Metal may rust, wood become rotten, or rope fray. This means that support posts, seats, climbing frames, swings, etc., may look safe but could snap at any time. They need constant inspection and repair.

- **poisonous plants, fruits and fungi:** many parents have no idea that several garden plants can cause severe symptoms or death. It is usually children who eat them thinking that they are edible. These are some of the ones to guard against:

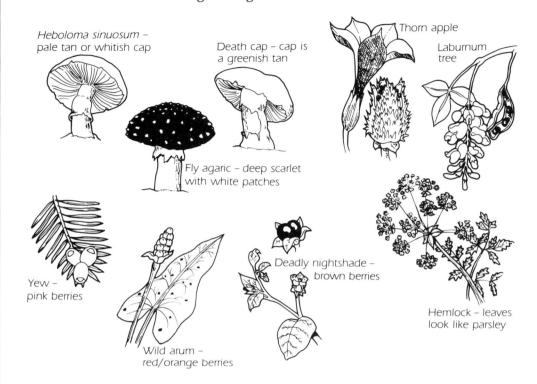

Hebeloma sinuosum –
pale tan or whitish cap

Death cap – cap is
a greenish tan

Thorn apple

Laburnum
tree

Fly agaric – deep scarlet
with white patches

Yew –
pink berries

Deadly nightshade –
brown berries

Wild arum –
red/orange berries

Hemlock – leaves
look like parsley

Poisonous plants and fungi

- **uneven surfaces:** many people have crazy paving, stone walls, decorative steps and paths. These usually begin to break up and become uneven after a few years and can be a real danger, especially to children and old people.

- **animals**, especially other people's, can be a nuisance in the garden. They can often get through a fence or gate and can frighten or attack small children. Also, animal droppings may cause disease if touched, and the germs then introduced into the human body.

- **compost heaps and garden fires** can be dangerous. The compost heap may contain harmful objects or substances. A fire may appear to be out but could blaze up again if touched by an inquisitive child.

These are some of the main dangers. Again it is young children, the handicapped and the elderly who are most at risk.

There are many potential dangers outside as well as inside the home. Accidents can happen anywhere and we can group the places where they are most likely to occur as follows:

- on the roads
- at school
- at work
- in the playground or recreation ground
- in the country
- 'out of bounds' areas such as building sites, railway embankments, electricity substations and reservoirs
- places involving water such as swimming pools, rivers, seaside, lakes and canals
- public places such as cinemas, public libraries, leisure centres and shops.

Accident fact file

Children dice with deat'

CHILDREN are dicing with death and running the risk of se
if they interfere with live electrical equipment, warns
Electricity.
Timing the warning with the long summer school holiday
more time on their hands, the
children to stay clear
e again appeal
verhead lines.

Climbers hurt
Thirteen climbers struck by lightning yesterday during a thunders'   n in the Italian Dolor'   rescued by heli-
co

Cuppa tragedy
A 78-year-old woman who set fire to herself while making a cup of tea died in hospital yesterday. Florence Collicott, of Fiennes Road, Rose Hill, Oxford, struck a match to light the gas and it went down the front of her dress.

Nine hurt as gale topples caravans
CONWY: Nine holidaymakers were injured early today, two seriously, when gale force winds blew over 14 caravans on an exposed seaside site.
Emergency services went to the Morfa Caravan Site at Conwy, North Wales, when the winds over'   the holiday caravans.
Fo   children were injured,
'sman. The injured
'ather and t'   'hree
'en '   '   at

Man loses leg
A man lost a leg when he fell in front of a London-bound express at Gloucester Station yesterday. He has not been named.

Hang-glide cras'
A hang-glider pilot was recovering in hospital after his craft smashed into a cliff and plunged hundreds of feet to the beach at Bossington, near Minehead, Somerset. James Greenshields, 28, from Henlade, near Taunton, has broken wrists, broken legs, a fractured pelvis and rib injuries.

Runawa lorry in blacks ra

Trench death
A workman was crushed to death when the wall of a trench collapsed on him at a building site in Portsmouth, Hants. He was Mr Henry Denton 48, of Dutton Lane, Eastleigh, near Southampton.

Fatal knock
Mrs Harriet Walker, 95, of Rectory Close, Burnham-on- Sea, Somerset, has died a week after suffering a broken hip when she was knocked down by a hit and run cyclist in St Andrew's churchyard in the town. The cyclist has not been traced.

These are the sorts of headlines we can see in our newspapers most days of the week.

1 Within your group, compile an *Accident Fact File* by collecting all the newspaper reports on different types of accidents which you can find. Do this for a month and then assess the results by considering the following questions:

a) Which are the commonest types of accidents?

b) Where do accidents usually take place – in the home, playground, factory, or on the roads?

c) Which age groups are most affected by which type of accident?

d) Do certain types of accident usually happen to males rather than females, or vice versa?

2 When you have the results of your survey, *evaluate* (see p. 173) the information and consider:

a) Are there any accident blackspots in your area?

b) Could more be done to educate young people in safety matters?

c) Are parents not taking sufficient responsibility for their children?

d) Could more be done to reduce the risks for old people?

ROAD SAFETY

5500 (including 500 children) killed per year

70 000 serious injuries per year

230 000 minor injuries per year

These numbers include:

	Killed	Injured
Pedestrians	1900	60 000
Pedal cyclists	300	30 000
Motor-cyclists	1000	63 000
Car users	2000	130 000

Within a year, the following will be involved in an accident:

1 *in every*

11	motor-scooter riders
16	motor-cycle riders
33	moped riders
37	heavy goods vehicle drivers
56	car drivers
78	light van drivers

These statistics show the number of deaths and people injured on the roads each year. These figures do not cover the whole scene as many injuries go unreported. Almost everybody can look back to a 'near miss' – a fall from a bicycle, a bump in a car, a dash across the road.

Fortunately the numbers of road accidents are dropping. This may be due to:

- people being made more safety conscious

- better training and teaching in schools on all matters of road safety

- media publicity such as TV programmes, articles in magazines, free leaflets, quizzes, etc.

- better safety designs for cars and other road vehicles

- the work of organisations such as RoSPA (see p. 88), the Health Education Authority, Child Accident Prevention Committee, and the use of the Tufty Club for the very young and the Green Cross Code for older children

- training schemes for cyclists and motor-cyclists

- the introduction of laws such as those which govern the wearing of seat belts, children travelling in the front seats of cars and speed restrictions

- the crackdown on drinking and driving

- the introduction of pedestrian areas and shopping precincts into towns, and the bypassing of towns and villages which sends heavy traffic round them instead of through them. This has been one of the most important methods of reducing accidents.

In 1981: 189 041 people were killed or injured in built-up areas;

59 191 were killed or injured in non-built-up areas.

In 1983: 188 183 people were killed or injured in built-up areas;

50 976 were killed or injured in non-built-up areas.

The road casualty figures in 1985 were the lowest since the Second World War, but we must not become too complacent about these facts. There are still over 75 000 people killed or severely injured on the roads every year:

THIS IS EQUAL TO THE SIZE OF A LARGE TOWN

Many of these casualties are children (14 and under).

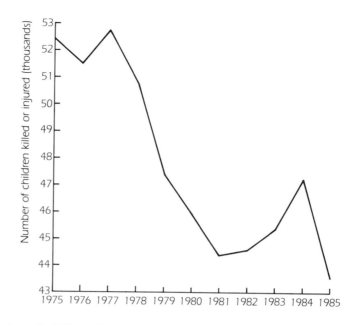

Number of children killed or injured on the roads in Britain

Study the chart above and answer these questions:

a) How many children were killed or injured from 1975 to 1985?

b) How many fewer children were affected in 1985 than in 1975?

c) In which year was there the largest increase in numbers?

d) In which year was there the largest drop in numbers?

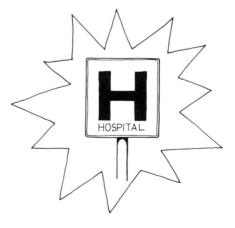

In 1983 there were 536 children killed on the roads. The chart opposite shows the ages of the children killed.

A First Home Economics Course

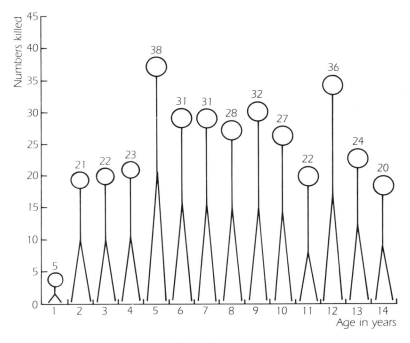

Children killed on the roads (1983)

Study the chart above and answer these questions:

a) Which age is at the most risk?

b) Which age is at the least risk?

c) Suggest some reasons for this.

d) Why do you think that a fairly high proportion of 12-year-olds are killed?

In 1980 the total number of children killed on the roads was 466. Let us see how some of these deaths were caused: 86 were riding bicycles; 8 were playing in the street; 170 ran into the road; 55 crossed the road without looking; 65 stepped from behind parked vehicles; 63 were car passengers.

Crossing the road without looking is very dangerous. Have you ever been so deeply involved in conversation that you forgot to look both ways? But worse still is running into the road – either unintentionally, as small children do, or during a game of chicken, to see who can run across the road and be the last in front of approaching traffic?

It is only stupid people who risk their lives for a dare or to show off. You should have been taught the 'Green Cross Code'.

1 This 'Green Cross Code' is in the wrong order. Rearrange it so that it is correct:

Look all around for traffic and listen.

When there is no traffic near, walk straight across the road.

Stand on the pavement near the kerb.

First find a safe place to cross, then stop.

Keep looking and listening for traffic while you cross.

If traffic is coming, let it pass. Look all around you again.

This sentence should help you:

Family Safety Lies In Warning Kiddies.

2 If you are a pedestrian or a road user, you should know the meaning of these traffic signs:

Traffic signs

Find out what they mean – a copy of the Highway Code will help you. Write a sentence to explain the meaning of each one.

Lots of things contribute to the numbers of road accidents. These include:

- time of day – whether it is dark, daylight or dusk; whether it is a quiet time or rush hour

- month of the year – whether children are at school or on holiday

- whether the road conditions are poor, e.g. snow, ice, wet or flood.

A First Home Economics Course

The charts below tell us some interesting facts and show us where and when we should be most careful.

A *Average number of casualties per hour per day (1983)*

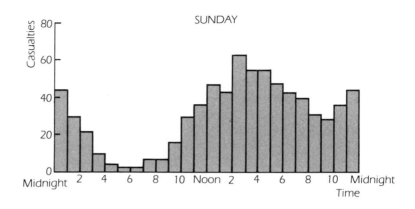

SUNDAY

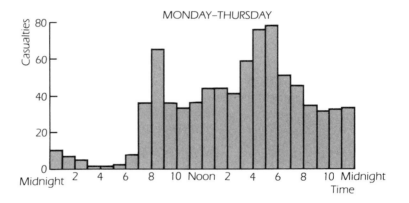

MONDAY–THURSDAY

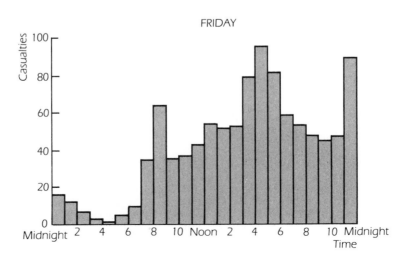

FRIDAY

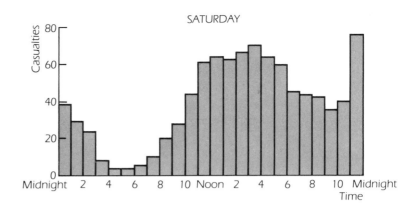

SATURDAY

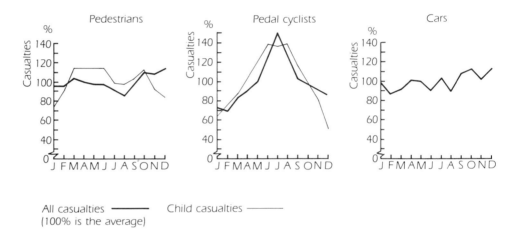

B *Monthly casualty figures for pedestrians – cyclists – cars (1983)*

Pedestrians

Pedal cyclists

Cars

All casualties ———— Child casualties ————
(100% is the average)

Chart **A** shows us that the most accidents occur:

Sundays   11–12 a.m. and 2–6 p.m.

Monday to 8–9 a.m. and 2–4 p.m.
Thursday

Friday   8–9 a.m., 3–6 p.m. and 11–12 midnight

Saturday   11 a.m.–6 p.m. and 11–12 midnight

Explain how these figures show the connection between accidents and:

• drinking and driving

• people going to and coming from work, school and shopping.

70

Chart **B** shows us how the monthly accident figures compare with each other. There is a sharp drop in the number of child pedestrian casualties in the winter months when children tend to stay indoors.

1 Why do you think that there is a drop in child pedestrian casualties during July, August and part of September, when it rises steeply again?

2 The same thing happens with cyclist casualties. Why are there many fewer casualties during the winter months with a peak of accidents in August?

3 Why do you think the line for car accidents is comparatively level?

Weather conditions

Conditions	Total number of casualties	
	Daylight	*Darkness*
Wet or flood	49 000	32 725
Snow or ice	5790	5230
Dry conditions	116 100	39 365

4 What information can you deduce from these figures? Remember, there is less traffic on the roads during the night and during bad weather conditions.

These are some of the main causes of road accidents:

to *pedestrians*
- inconsiderate and uncaring road users; vehicles which are going too fast, vehicles badly parked, cyclists riding on the pavement
- vehicles which are not in roadworthy condition with poor brakes, worn tyres or faulty lights
- inexperienced drivers; those who do not know what to do in an emergency, do not know the Highway Code, or have had insufficient practice
- those who are breaking the law; speeding drivers, learner drivers driving without an experienced instructor, drivers who have been drinking or taking drugs
- children who have not been taught road safety

- children who are too young to be on the roads alone
- older children playing in the street; playing ball games, doing 'dares', being too boisterous, not concentrating on safety
- people who are physically unwell or handicapped and have slow movements and reactions
- elderly people who cannot move quickly, have slower reactions, and panic in an emergency.

to *cyclists*

- other traffic not making allowances for the cyclist; passing too close, pulling out in front of him too quickly, stopping sharply in front of him
- animals running unexpectedly into the cyclist's path
- icy road conditions; fog, snow, greasy patches on the roads
- dusk – just before it gets dark when visibility is poor
- inexperience and ignorance of the Highway Code and the rules of the road
- riding a bike carelessly; without holding the handlebars, carrying a passenger on the crossbar or on the back, showing off
- faulty brakes, tyres, lights
- carrying too many parcels or weighty objects which affect the balance of the bike
- wearing clothing which trails or flaps; long scarves or baggy trousers
- hanging on to the tailboard of lorries
- going too fast, not giving sufficient braking distance
- the bike too big or small for the rider
- turning off without checking the traffic properly.

discussion area

– The most dangerous ages for cyclists are 12 to 14 years.
– Five times as many boys get hurt as girls.
Suggest some reasons for these two facts.

to *motorbike and moped riders*

Many of the hazards which apply to cyclists also apply to powered bikes. Many youngsters start riding motorbikes before they are mature and sensible enough to use them properly. They use them as a status symbol to show off to their friends and boost their own ego.

Many of them do not learn to drive them properly and they blatantly break the law over speeding, dangerous machines, carrying passengers whilst still learning, etc.

A First Home Economics Course

These are the main causes of accidents:

- speed; going too fast for the road and traffic conditions
- inexperienced and incompetent driving
- drinking and driving
- using heavily tinted or scratched visors
- wearing an all dark outfit so that they do not show up in poor visibility.

Fatal and serious injuries to motor cyclists

Age	No. of accidents
16	1606
17–19	8858
20–29	5922
30–39	1543
40–49	782

These figures show that it is those in the teenager and twenties age groups who are most at risk. Many are crippled for life, many injure other people as well as themselves.

to *car drivers and passengers*

Many of the previous points also apply to cars. Additional dangers are:

- inexperienced and careless driving
- disregard for safety; not using seat belts, being distracted by loud music and dangling objects on windscreen
- driving a car which is in a dangerous condition
- allowing animals to be unrestrained in the car
- allowing children to misbehave and be distracting – they should be comfortable, restrained and occupied
- driving too aggressively with little concern for other road users
- having poor eyesight, slow reactions
- being under stress, taking medication, being in poor health.

What can *we* do to avoid road accidents?

These are useful ways of reducing the risks:

- learn the Green Cross Code and the Highway Code
- take advantage of the appropriate training courses, e.g. the National Cycling Proficiency Test, motorbike training schemes, advanced driving tests such as those set by the Institute of Advanced Motorists
- think safe and be alert to danger at all times
- do not take any risks, do not show off, behave sensibly
- check your vehicle regularly and have repairs carried out straight away

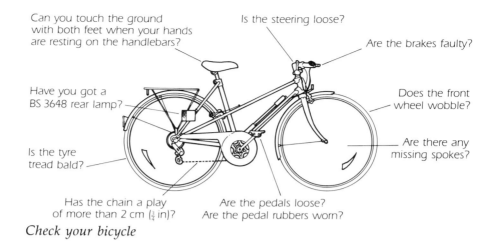

Can you touch the ground with both feet when your hands are resting on the handlebars?

Is the steering loose?

Are the brakes faulty?

Have you got a BS 3648 rear lamp?

Does the front wheel wobble?

Is the tyre tread bald?

Are there any missing spokes?

Has the chain a play of more than 2 cm ($\frac{3}{4}$ in)?

Are the pedals loose?
Are the pedal rubbers worn?

Check your bicycle

- remember – speed kills; someone walking can stop a lot more quickly than a moving vehicle can
- pedestrians should always use a pedestrian crossing if possible
- quiet country lanes can be just as dangerous as busy streets; they tend to have a lot of bends and vehicles are often travelling too fast, they may have a bumpy surface hazardous to cyclists, there may be unsighted, slow vehicles coming out of gates
- wear safety clothing where necessary.

Safety wear

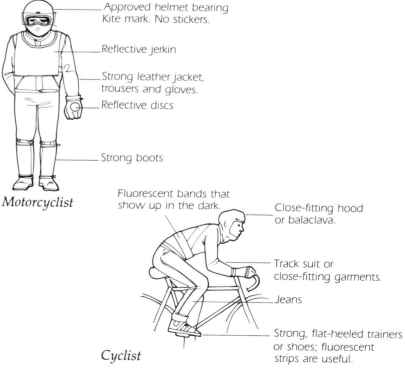

Approved helmet bearing Kite mark. No stickers.

Reflective jerkin

Strong leather jacket, trousers and gloves.

Reflective discs

Strong boots

Motorcyclist

Fluorescent bands that show up in the dark.

Close-fitting hood or balaclava.

Track suit or close-fitting garments.

Jeans

Strong, flat-heeled trainers or shoes; fluorescent strips are useful.

Cyclist

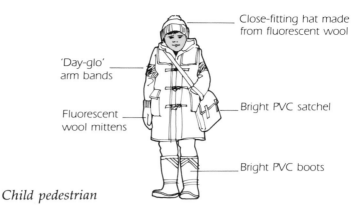

- Close-fitting hat made from fluorescent wool
- 'Day-glo' arm bands
- Bright PVC satchel
- Fluorescent wool mittens
- Bright PVC boots

Child pedestrian

- make use of the safety equipment and gadgets which are available.

Safety equipment

On the roads
  a) *Fluorescent coats for dogs*
  b) *Fluorescent legbands for horses*
  c) *Walking reins for child pedestrians*

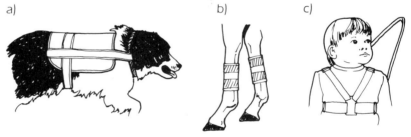

a)   b)   c)

In the car
  a) *Carrycot safety belts*
  b) *Child's back seat*
  c) *Seat belts – back and front*
  d) *Air bags which inflate on impact*
  e) *Back facing baby seat*
  f) *Child safety locks*

a)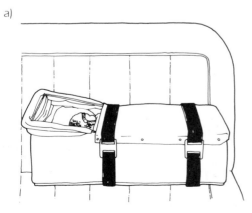

b)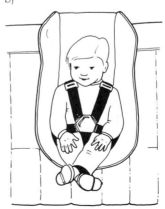

continued

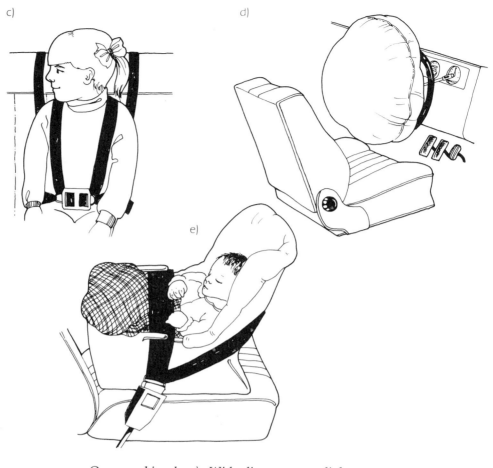

On your bicycle a) *Wide diameter rear light*
b) *Spacer bar fitted to a rear wheel*
c) *Bicycle rear view mirror*
d) *Reflectors on pedals.*

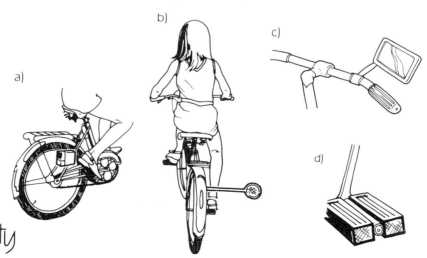

a) Describe how all these safety features help to protect us.
b) Try to discover other safety features for road users.

A First Home Economics Course

Special points for the elderly

Pedestrians who are at most risk of death or serious injury are in the 70 and over age group. The 60 to 69 age group also has a high risk factor.

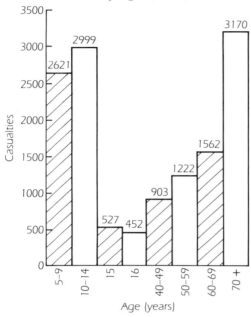

Fatal and serious casualties – by age (1983)

Analysis

Which group is most at risk?
Which age group is least at risk?
What is the total number of casualties under 17?
What is the total number of casualties 60 and over?
To which age group do you belong?
Are you at high or low risk?
From the factors given in this section and your own research try to give some reasons why these figures are as they are.

(Road Accident Statistics RoSPA)

The possible reasons for older people being in a high risk category include:

- their hearing and eyesight may not be as acute
- they may become less mobile and slow on their feet
- their reactions in an emergency may be slower
- they may take risks thinking that others should wait for them
- they may become very nervous in traffic and become hesitant
- they may be slower to make decisions and less positive in their actions
- they may not be aware of new road signs, crossing procedures and regulations.

What can the elderly do to help *themselves*?

- use and understand Pelican and Zebra crossings
- avoid going out if possible during rush hour traffic
- always use spectacles or hearing aid if they are needed
- avoid going out in icy, foggy or snowy conditions unless it is essential
- wait until the road is clear before crossing; if necessary ask for help

- do not think that drivers will automatically stop for an elderly person. People can stop quicker than traffic.
- if it is necessary to go out at night, wear or carry something white, e.g. a scarf, handbag, or newspaper.

What can the *community* do to help elderly pedestrians?

- be aware of them – car drivers, cyclists and motorcyclists must be aware of the limitations of elderly people. There are 10 million over 60's.
- be ready to help if you see them hesitating at the kerb or in difficulties on the pavement
- do not push or jostle in your haste to cross the road or get past them
- look out for the road signs which indicate that elderly or handicapped people may be about and slow down
- show patience and concern.

SAFETY AT SCHOOL

Accidents will happen wherever there are:

- crowded rooms and corridors
- large numbers of people pushing and jostling and in a hurry
- buildings designed to accomodate far fewer people
- potential dangers such as staircases, swing doors, polished floors, large windows
- equipment used for craft, science and PE
- people who are careless of their own and other people's safety.

Many of these circumstances will apply to your own school. Accidents need not happen if you follow a few basic rules:
  i) take heed of the general rules for safety in the school and those which concern specialist rooms
  ii) do not rush about
  iii) do not be tempted to show off just to impress your friends
  iv) wear sensible shoes which are safe and will not slip, and clothing which will not get caught in doors
  v) use a well designed, large bag for your possessions; do not try to carry too much at once
  vi) do not tamper with electrical or gas appliances, machinery of any sort, chemicals or PE equipment
  vii) do not lean out of windows or over banisters
  viii) act responsibly – your life or someone else's may depend upon it.

These are the type of accidents which happen at school – can you add to the list?

- broken bones or bruising caused by falling downstairs
- head injuries from falling over banisters or objects dropped from upper floors
- hands and fingers trapped in windows and doors
- bites from animals in the biology laboratory
- cuts from sharp knives and equipment in craft rooms
- burns from using cookers, bunsen burners, welding equipment
- broken toes caused when heavy objects are dropped
- car and bicycle accidents from vehicles in the parking area or cycle sheds.

There are many more, but they need not happen if you are careful.

These are all striking safety posters produced by RoSPA.

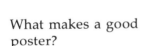

What makes a good poster?

- Good colour
- Clear outline
- Humour
- No unnecessary words
- Large enough to see

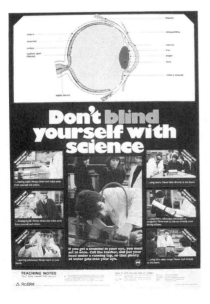

Safety in schools

Design a poster to illustrate one of these possible danger areas in your school:

steep flights of stairs

congested corridors

swing doors

science laboratory

craft rooms

hard surface play area

See if you can get permission to put the posters up on the walls round the school.

SAFETY AT WORK

There are just under 700 fatal accidents at work every year in Great Britain. (RoSPA figures for 1982).

There are 400 000 notifiable accidents at work each year (estimated numbers).

There are many more minor accidents which go unreported. Work is a dangerous place to be unless you are careful and follow the rules. The greatest number of accidents occur in mines and quarries, followed by construction sites, the gas, electricity and water industries and agriculture.

Why do you think these have the highest risk factor?

The most usual injuries sustained include: finger, thumb or part of limbs amputated; fractured and dislocated limbs; injuries to eyes; cuts and bruises; broken or bruised toes; burns.

Every place of work is covered by the Health and Safety at Work Act (1974) which deals with:

- general points for health and safety at work
- the duty of employers to ensure the health and safety of their employees
- the protection of every employer and employee at any place of work.

80

These are some of the factors which will help to prevent accidents at work:

- thorough training of all employees in safety procedures
- regular inspections carried out on machinery, appliances and buildings, and repairs carried out immediately
- provision and compulsory wearing of safety clothing and use of safety equipment such as safety boots, safety belts
- a Health and Safety Officer at every place of work; larger concerns will need a safety team
- first aid equipment easily available and some trained first aid officers
- provision of fire extinguishers; emergency exits kept clear; fire doors kept closed; sand and water available; emergency telephone available.

The employee can help by:

- being aware of danger at all times and being safety conscious
- knowing and carrying out the safety rules
- not going to work if he is ill or under the influence of drugs or alcohol which will put him or others at risk
- acting in a sensible fashion and not fooling about
- being careful with matches, cigarette ends and litter
- taking care with tools, storage of poisons and chemicals and electrical appliances.

If everyone played their part, there would be fewer accidents.

Match these items of safety wear to the people on p. 82 you think they would be most useful to:

1 Hard helmet   2 Bright yellow PVC jacket   3 Safety boots with strengthened toe plate   4 Safety goggles

5 Riding hat   6 Long leather boots   7 Ear muffs   8 Prote...

A School child   B Road worker   C Builder

D Foundry worker   E Motorcyclist   F Jockey

SAFETY AT PLAY

Many of the things we do in our leisure time include an element of danger. Human beings enjoy taking risks and many sporting activities demand courage and endurance, BUT there is no sense in endangering your life just to try and prove that you can climb a very high tree, swim across a river or go down a deep pothole. Sporting activities claim at least 100 lives a year.

- Learn all you can about any sport before you start and understand the safety procedures.
- Get advice and tuition from an expert.
  Never use equipment which is too big, too small, too powerful or too complicated for your size and experience.
  `lways let others know where and when you are going
  nbing, swimming, walking etc.

  ̇ groups or with a friend, if possible with an
  ̇nced leader.

  ̇ other people's safety as well as your own and
  ̇le who may have to try and rescue you if you
  ̇lties.

  ̇T DO IT!

Safety in sport

1 What type of accidents can happen during these sporting activities?

2 How can these accidents be avoided?

3 Describe an accident which happened to you or a member of your family whilst you were involved in a sporting activity.

4 Complete these two limericks:
There was a young fellow called Ian
Who was keen to learn all about skiing,
He _ _ _ _ _ _ _ _ _ _ _ _ _ _ _ _ _ _ _
_ _ _ _ _ _ _ _ _ _ _ _ _ _ _ _ _ _ _
_ _ _ _ _ _ _ _ _ _ _ _ _ _ _ _ _ _

There was a young lady called Glenys
Who was very proficient at tennis,
She _ _ _ _ _ _ _ _ _ _ _ _ _ _ _ _ _ _
_ _ _ _ _ _ _ _ _ _ _ _ _ _ _ _ _ _
_ _ _ _ _ _ _ _ _ _ _ _ _ _ _ _ _ _

Sport should be fun; it should be healthy.

It should not endanger life.

SAFETY ON THE WATER

Nearly 500 people (including 100 children under 15) accidentally drown in Great Britain every year. Many more people would drown but for the help of others.

Many of these accidental drownings occur near home.

Some of the victims could have been saved if their rescuers had been skilled in resuscitation.

A higher proportion of males than females are involved in drowning or near-drowning accidents. At most risk of drowning are 5 to 10-year-olds, followed by the 1 to 5 age group. 10 to 14-year-olds are involved in the highest number of accidents involving near-drowning. Most accidents occur at rivers, swimming pools, canals and the sea. Disused quarries, water tanks, potholes and wells all claim lives also.

Ten lives were lost fishing; boating and canoeing claimed nine lives; water sports claimed ten; and sailing, five lives in 1982.

These are frightening figures. Many deaths could be avoided if all children were taught to swim – the younger the better. Most swimming pools offer family sessions or toddler-parent sessions and most schools offer swimming tuition.

How safe are you in, on, or near water?

1 **Water safety quiz** – which are correct answers?

1. A buoyancy vest or life-jacket is **essential/desirable** for children in an open boat.

2. Children should not play with air beds in the sea. **TRUE   FALSE**

3. If you accidentally fall into deep water, remove as much heavy clothing as possible. **TRUE   FALSE**

4. If you see someone in difficulty in the water, immediately jump in to the rescue. **TRUE   FALSE**

5. A child can drown in **seconds/minutes/hours**.

6. A water butt in a garden should always have a lid. **TRUE   FALSE**

7. If a boat you are in overturns, hang on to it until rescued. **TRUE   FALSE**

8. A beach which is dangerous will have warning signs such as a red flag. **TRUE   FALSE**

9. Children should be instructed never to play on towpaths or by the side of a canal. **TRUE   FALSE**

10. Children should **always/sometimes/never** go fishing alone.

11. Iced-over ponds are safe to walk on as long as you keep to the sides. **TRUE   FALSE**

12. Which of these would you do if you saw someone drowning and you could not swim?

   — Throw something such as a piece of wood, lifebelt or rubber tyre into the water.
   — Shout loudly for help.
   — Send someone to dial 999 or get some other help.
   — Try to reach the person with a stick, pole or rope and hang on until help arrives.

Now check your score with the answers on p. 95.

2 Review and assess the methods of presenting safety measures: posters – TV adverts – radio warnings – comics, magazines, newspapers – booklets and leaflets – talks to groups and organisations – films.

Which are the most successful methods? Why?

3 All these posters (produced by RoSPA) get over a safety message.

a) To which age group is each poster most important?

b) Explain the message behind each one.

c) Which one would catch your attention quickly and why?

Safety poster analysis

4 Explain some of the dangers connected with:

- inadequately fenced-off railway tracks and automatic train barriers
- electricity pylons and overhead wires
- parks and recreation grounds
- disused and derelict buildings
- building sites
- reservoirs
- marshy areas.

Here are some key words to help you:
warning lights, barriers, quiet electric trains, speed, kites, wind, ice, dogs, broken glass, splinters, builders' equipment, vermin, hoists and lifts, rotten wood, quicksand.

PEOPLE AND ORGANISATIONS WHO LOOK AFTER OUR SAFETY

activity

Some people spend a lot of time helping us to keep safe. These are some of the people whose job is SAFETY.

Policewoman

Traffic warden

Fireman

Ambulance woman

Lollipop person

Road safety officer

People who look after our safety

1 Do you know anyone who has this sort of job?

2 Put yourself in their place and write an interesting account entitled 'A day in the life of . . . (a lollipop person, traffic warden etc.)

There are also lots of organisations which deal with safety. The main one is **RoSPA** – the Royal Society for the Prevention of Accidents. This society is the largest in Europe dealing with safety matters. It gives advice, information, publicity and training. It helps with consumer safety and education, and it produces figures (statistics) to show where the main accident trends lie. These are some more groups which help to protect us.

Royal National Lifeboat Institution

British Safety Council

St John Ambulance Association

English Schools Swimming Association

British Standards Institute

British Red Cross Society

Fire Protection Association

The Health Education Authority (previously known as the Health Education Council)

SAFETY AND THE LAW

One of the top Government priorities is to protect public health and safety. Apart from the cost in human suffering to both the victim and his family, accidents cost a lot of money to the tax payer.

These figures are a rough guide to the amount of money which accidents consume:

Official estimates of accident costs – 1983

Cost to the NHS of:
Home accidents	– £50 million per year
Occupational accidents and diseases	– £2000 million to £3000 million per year
Road accidents	– £2378 million per year

The average cost per road casualty is:

	1977	1983
Fatal casualty	£56 700	£150 040
Serious casualty	£3380	£6950
Slight casualty	£80	£170
Average	£1930	£4370

These figures include all the services and personnel needed to deal with an accident, e.g. police, ambulancemen, firemen; cost of hospital treatment; loss of earnings, etc.

How is the Government trying to reduce the number of accidents and improve safety conditions?

- Education – safety education in schools, places of work, public libraries, leisure centres, local government offices, clinics, hospitals and health centres, and through public services such as gas and electricity. By means of posters, leaflets, TV programmes, videos, quizzes, competitions, radio and magazines. By getting to the people most at risk – children, elderly, handicapped, and workers.

- By liaison with manufacturers, retailers and commerce to encourage the introduction and maintenance of safety standards.

- By co-operation and financial help for voluntary bodies, e.g. RoSPA, the British Red Cross Society, etc. who are concerned with health and safety.

- By training and providing safety officers and personnel.

- By legislation – that is, making laws to protect us from danger, and to help us to protect ourselves.

These laws govern things which happen:

i) on the roads, covering such things as seat belts, speeding restrictions, lights on bicycles, MOT inspections and the wearing of crash helmets.

ii) in factories, shops, public buildings; such as the use of building materials, safety guards for machinery, provision of protective clothing, limited working hours, safety of lifts, stairs, ramps and efficient lighting.

iii) in the environment; such as the control of insecticides, air and water pollution, lead in the atmosphere, sewage disposal, dumping of chemicals and waste.

iv) in the home; it is difficult for the Government to pass laws about what we do in the home, but they can control the standards of things we buy. This is called 'consumer protection'. 'The Consumer Safety Act' 1978 gives the Government the power to control the safety of household products. Toys, electrical goods, cooking utensils, upholstered furniture and nightwear are just some of the things included.

How well do you know the Law?

TRUE or FALSE?

1. You must have a bicycle rear lamp made to British Standards.

2. It is illegal to cycle with a small child on the crossbar.

3. You must stop your vehicle at a pedestrian crossing, even if there are no pedestrians on it.

4. A bicycle must have two brakes.

5. Helmets must be worn by motorcyclists but need not be worn by pillion passengers.

6. Seat belts must always be used in the front seat of a car.

7. If the traffic light shows only amber, the next colour will be red.

8. A car must have an MOT test every 3 years after the first three years.

9. A cyclist can be prosecuted for riding when under the influence of drink or drugs.

10. Prams and pushchairs must be made of materials which are harmless to children.

11. An electric fire must have a guard on it but a gas fire need not.

12. Children's ready-made nightwear must be made from material which does not burn or flare easily.

13. It is illegal to leave a child under the age of 12 years in a room where there is an unguarded fire.

14. All toys sold in this country must comply with Government regulations.

15. All public buildings must comply with fire regulations.

(See p. 95 for answers.)

These laws are made to protect us – there would be fewer accidents if everybody obeyed them.

A First Home Economics Course

FIRST AID

Accident **prevention** is the best thing, but unfortunately there are always going to be some accidents.

Accidents usually happen very quickly, it is best to be prepared and to know what to do and how to cope in an emergency.

There are some general rules which apply:

- Do not panic. A little blood goes a long way and many accidents are not nearly as bad as they first appear.
- Act quickly – sensible, speedy action can save lives.
- Remove the victim from the source of danger, without endangering yourself.
- Make the casualty comfortable. Stay with them if possible. Get help by dialling 999 or send someone else for help.
- Unless you know about first aid, you can do more harm than good. Do not move the casualty unless he or she is in danger.
- Do not give the casualty anything to eat or drink.
- Bleeding must be stopped (see p. 92, breathing must be started by mouth-to-mouth resuscitation if necessary. Check that air passages are not obstructed.
- Try to be calm and reassure the casualty.
- A person may appear to be all right after an accident, but may suffer from delayed shock or may have injuries which are not obvious. Always get medical attention to be sure.
- You will feel more secure and self-confident and be of greater help if you have a basic knowledge of first aid and an up-to-date first aid kit. Your first aid kit should always: be kept clean; be kept in a strong, labelled container with a lid; be kept in an accessible place which everyone knows; be regularly checked to replace used items and throw away out of date stock.

Your kit should contain:

Contents of a first aid kit

First aid procedures

Basic first aid

Injury	What to do in an emergency	Special Points
BURNS AND SCALDS	Put the burn under cold running water for at least ten minutes. Cover the burn loosely with a non-fluffy cloth, take the person to hospital.	Do not put butter or ointment on a burn. Do not try to remove fabric stuck to the skin.
SCALDS	The same treatment as burns. Clothes covering the scald can be removed.	
CHOKING	For a baby or small child – hold child upside-down by the legs and give a sharp slap between shoulder blades. Older person – tip forward from the waist, sharp slap on the back.	Do not try to remove the object with the fingers, you may push it further in.
SUFFOCA-TION	Take away the cause of the suffocation. Give mouth-to-mouth resuscitation if breathing has stopped.	
CUTS	For severe bleeding, press firmly on the wound with a pad of clean cloth or fingers. Continue until bleeding stops. Raise the injured limb. Apply a clean dressing. Go to hospital for treatment.	Wounds occurring outdoors may need tetanus injection. Do not try to use a tourniquet.
DROWNING	Remove person from water, give mouth-to-mouth resuscitation if breathing has stopped.	Do not give up too soon. Breathing can restart up to 1 hour afterwards.

continued

A First Home Economics Course

FALLS	Children usually re-cover quickly, elderly people often fracture or break bones. Do not move the person, get help quickly.	Observe for some hours afterwards for shock and after-effects.
BROKEN OR FRACTURED BONES	Do not move the limb or body unless it is essential. Make the casualty comfortable and get help.	
POISONING	Look for the pills or liquid which caused the accident. Take the person to hospital taking the poison (or empty bottle) with you. Only give milk or water to drink if the cause was turpentine, petrol, acids or caustics.	Do not try to make the person sick.
ELECTRIC SHOCK	Switch off the current. Give mouth-to-mouth resuscitation. Get help quickly. There may be burns also.	Check that your hands are dry.

First aid knowledge should be kept up-to-date as new methods and procedures are always being tried out and perfected.

More detailed information and practical experience can be obtained from:

- The British Red Cross Society
- St John Ambulance (England and Wales); St Andrews (Scotland)
- Royal Life Saving Society
- Scouts or Guides
- your local hospital.

Find out the details about joining the British Red Cross Society or the St John Ambulance Association – your public library should be able to help you.

ROLE-PLAY

What would *you* do?

Here are six situations when an accident has occurred or is happening:

a) A child drinking bleach.

b) A small child hanging out of an open upper-storey window.

c) An elderly man fallen down stairs.

d) Mother cut her hand when cutting a loaf of bread.

e) Someone in difficulties in the river.

f) A rider fallen off her horse in a quiet country lane.

If possible, act out these situations with other members of your group.

What would you do – if you were with someone else or if you were by yourself when you saw these things happen?

Think of some more accident situations and work out the procedures you would take.

> **For your HEALTH'S sake – be SAFE!**

Answers to quiz on p. 85

Answer scheme (number of marks in brackets).
1. essential (*1*)   2. True (*1*)   3. False (*1*)–Remove heavy shoes, but clothing will keep air trapped against the body and help to reduce hypothermia.   4. False (*1*)
5. All three (*3*)   6. True (*1*)   7. True (*1*) If you try to swim for the shore you could drown.   8. True (*1*)   9. True (*1*)   10. Never (*1*)   11. False (*1*)   12. Any or all of them (*4*).

TOTAL: 17 marks. Add 3 marks if you have taken a life-saving course, add 5 marks if you can carry out mouth to mouth resuscitation. FINAL TOTAL 25 marks.

Answers to quiz on p. 90

1. True   2. True   3. False   4. True   5. False   6. True
7. True   8. False   9. True   10. True   11. False   12. True
13. True   14. True   15. True

Find out the correct answers to the questions where a *false* answer is given.

Health and Food

A HEALTHY, VARIED DIET

Many of us are not as fit or as healthy as we could be because we do not have a satisfactory diet.

Knowing about the value of food and sensible eating in a healthy lifestyle is important. For a healthy diet we need to know how to:

- make the correct choice of food
- decide how much food to eat
- prepare and cook food carefully.

The results of a poor diet could be:
MALNUTRITION, STARVATION or DISEASE.

These problems occur where food shortages are commonplace. Find out more about these nutritional problems.

- What is the name that we give to the food we choose to eat each day?

Some people may need to eat a special **diet** to maintain their level of health and fitness, e.g. diabetics who eat a carbohydrate controlled diet; coeliacs who eat a gluten-free diet.

A healthy, varied diet will:

- keep us alive
- keep the body active and fit
- help us to grow properly
- be enjoyable.

CHOOSING FOOD

Eating to live is important to us all.

Look at these reasons for choosing food:

- it looks nice
- it is quick to eat

- you know it is a healthy food
- it was recently advertised on TV
- it is your favourite food
- it does not cost very much
- you are hungry
- everybody else is eating it
- it is what you always eat
- it is quick to prepare.

Which do you think are important for healthy living?

There may be other reasons for choosing particular foods to eat, e.g. religious and personal beliefs. A good selection of foods will contribute towards a healthy, varied diet.

All foods are made up of **nutrients** which work together to keep the body healthy. Many foods contain more than one nutrient. If the food supplies a large quantity of one or several nutrients, it can be classed as a main food source of those particular nutrients. For example, liver is a main source of protein *and* iron. Each nutrient has specific functions:

- to help us to grow and to keep the body structure well maintained
- to keep us warm and give us enough energy to work and play
- to keep us fit, healthy and in good working order.

E	T	N	A		B	T	N		X	O	W
I	T	O	U	U	E	W	U	O	V		V
Z	F	A	T	D	V	C	T	R	H	E	I
	M	E	R	F		T	R	D	B	F	T
S	I		C	D	B	E	I	A	F	B	A
A	N	G	F	M	Y	N	T	F	G		M
Q	E	R	O	N	K	H	I	B	H	A	I
D	R	L	P	I	P	R	O	T	E	I	N
K	A		J	J	X		N	B	O		S
A	L	K	L	Y	M	O	N	I	R	P	T
K	S	L	I	B	Q	P		G	Y	A	Z
M	E		Q	R	C	S	J	S	H	R	C

Look at this wordsearch and find out the names of the five main nutrients. Also hidden is the name given to the study of the nutrients. What is it? (Words may run across, up, down, or diagonally.)

NUTRITIONAL VALUE

What do these nutrients do? Look at the chart below:

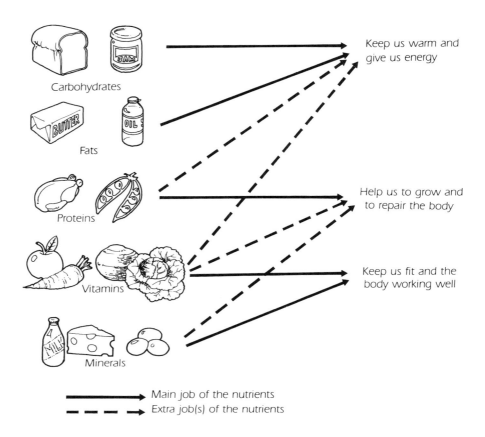

The diet must also contain water and dietary fibre – both are needed for the normal everyday functioning of the body.

Water – is needed in every body cell and for processes such as digestion to take place. About 70 per cent of the body is made up of water.

Dietary fibre – adds bulk to the food and helps waste to be excreted from the body efficiently.

Try to eat a selection of foods from each of the groups on the next page every day to give you a healthy, varied diet. Your appetite will be a reasonable guide to the amount of food to eat but it will not help you to choose the right foods or be completely accurate about how much to eat.

A First Home Economics Course

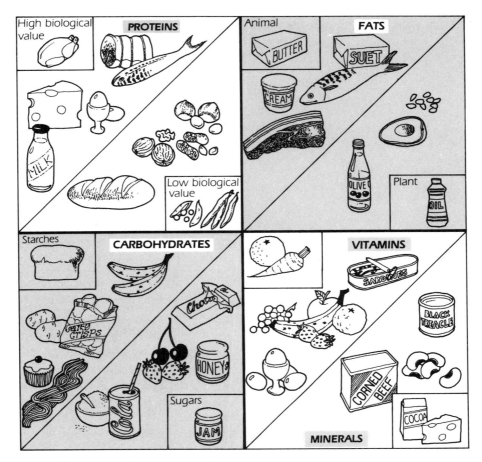

Facts about the nutrients

Nutrient	Facts
Protein	• The body cannot store protein. • Proteins of high biological value contain all the essential amino acids, e.g. meat, eggs, fish, soya. • Proteins of low biological value do not contain all the essential amino acids but can be eaten together to 'complement' each other and provide enough essential amino acids, e.g. beans on toast. • Teenagers need 58–75 g protein each day.
Carbohydrate	• Starches and sugars are high energy foods. • Sugar is sometimes called an 'empty' energy food (no other nutritional value). • Too much carbohydrate, in excess of energy needs, can be changed to fat and stored in the body. *continued*

Nutrient	Facts
	• All carbohydrates must first be broken down during digestion to glucose to be used as energy in the body.
Fat	• Saturated fats are mainly from animal sources and are usually solid at room temperature. • Unsaturated fats are mainly from plant sources and are usually liquid at room temperature. • Fats may be visible or invisible in food. • Fats are made up of fatty acids and glycerol. Some fatty acids are essential.

The above nutrients all provide energy for the voluntary and involuntary actions of the body (see p. 108).

Nutrient	Facts
Vitamins	• Each vitamin is different and cannot be replaced by any other one. They are only required in small amounts. • Vitamins A, D, E and K are fat-soluble and can be stored in the body. • Vitamin C and those in the B group are water-soluble and cannot be stored in the body. • Some vitamins can be made in the body. Some vitamins enable other nutrients to do their work efficiently. (Find out the proper names of the vitamins.)
Minerals	• Mineral elements are present in a wide variety of foods in varying amounts and are essential for the healthy working of the cells and body fluids. • To have too much or too little of some minerals can contribute to specific diseases. • The minerals which the body requires in *very* small quantities are called 'trace' elements, e.g. fluoride. • The amounts needed of certain minerals may be affected by our age, type of work, state of health and climate, e.g. a good supply of calcium is essential during pregnancy.

Try to find some foods which have been fortified with vitamins and/or minerals. Why have they been included?

activity

For your notebook make a table like the one below:

Food groups	Foods	🙂	😐	🙁
High biological value protein	Lean meats Liver/kidney Chicken/turkey Eggs Milk and its products Hard cheeses			
Low biological value protein	Peas, beans, lentils (pulses) Nuts Bread Potato			
Animal fats	Cream Hard cheeses Butter Fatty meat (bacon) Oily fish (mackerel)			
Plant oils	Nuts Margarine Fruit Vegetables			
Starch	Wholemeal bread Potato Wholewheat pasta Brown rice Cakes and pastries			
Sugars	Chocolate Jam/marmalade Cakes			
Vitamins	Sweets Oily fish (mackerel) Cereals and their products Vegetables and fruit Yeast extract			
Minerals	Lean meat (corned beef) Green vegetables Cheese			

Key 🙂 = a very good source

😐 = quite a good source

🙁 = not a very good source

These symbols indicate the nutritional level of the foods listed in the chart. Put a √ in the appropriate column.

Some of the minor ailments we suffer from may be due to poor eating habits. Such things as: ● poor skin conditions ● bad teeth and breath ● indigestion ● constipation ● dull, out of condition hair.

Many illnesses can also result from either eating too much of the wrong foods or eating too little of the right foods.

Some people may develop a food allergy, e.g. a rash, swellings or other symptoms may occur.

DIETARY GOALS

Research has led to the introduction of dietary goals. Their aim is to guide us in the choice of healthy foods. The main ones are:

A To eat less fat. Too much fat can cause heart disease and obesity.
B To eat less sugar. Too much sugar can cause dental problems and obesity.
C To eat less salt. Too much salt can affect blood pressure and cause heart problems.
D To eat more unrefined foods. Too little fibre can cause digestive problems.

Other important dietary considerations include:

● the importance of breast feeding
● drinking less alcohol
● sufficient and varied amounts of protein
● eating foods with fewer additives.

1 Explain why these are also important for healthy living.

2 These charts show how our diet *should* be changing.

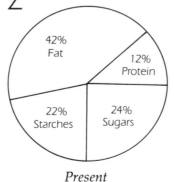

Present

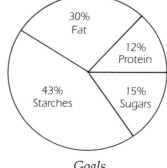

Goals

Convert these figures into a bar chart to indicate our present diet and dietary goals.

A First Home Economics Course

The NACNE report published dietary goals. What does the abbreviation NACNE mean? Find out which other reports recommend changes in our diet.

Study the pie charts and then answer these questions:

a) Why would you expect children in the future to have fewer dental problems?

b) How will the higher percentage of carbohydrate affect the health of the body?

c) How will these goals affect obesity?

3 Now make a list of all the food you ate and drank yesterday using a chart like the one shown here. Describe your food intake and use a √ to show which dietary goals it achieves.

Meal	Foods	Main nutrients	Dietary goals			
			A	B	C	D
Breakfast						
Snack						
Midday meal						
Snack						
Evening Meal						
Snack						

4 What changes would make your diet more in keeping with the dietary goals?

EATING PATTERNS

Many families prefer to plan their own daily meal timetable to match their lifestyle and culture.

This could be a typical plan of main meals:

Breakfast
Midday meal
Evening meal

Complete a class survey about eating patterns. Fill in a questionnaire like this:

A How many meals do you eat each day? ☐

B Do you eat breakfast regularly? Yes ☐ No ☐

C Why do you think it important to start the day with a nutritious breakfast? . . . .
. . . .
. . . .

D Is your main meal of the day eaten at midday or in the evening? ☐ ☐
Midday Evening

E Does your family try to eat at least one meal a day together? Yes ☐ No ☐

F Which is this meal usually? . . . .

G Do you rely on between meal snacks to fill you up? Yes ☐ No ☐

- Make a summary of the results.
- What are your conclusions?
- Have you noticed any cultural differences in your group?
- How many people have snacks between meals?

Think about why you eat snacks between meals.

Snacks can cause over-weight – they are often high in sugar and fat.
They may be too filling and spoil the appetite for proper meals.

BUT

snacks can be nutritious if chosen carefully and not eaten too often between meals.

Last year, in Britain, fast food sales were worth £2200 million. Fish and chips were still our favourite take-away food with sales of £600 million, according to a recent survey.

Take-away meals or fast foods can be bought and consumed quickly, away from home or at home.

1

a) Which of these do you have in your area? Are there others you could add?

b) Ask how many people in your class eat take-away food? (Often; Sometimes; Never).

c) List some reasons for eating take-away food.

d) Why should we not eat this type of food too often?

2 John and his two friends are coming home from a visit to the local swimming baths. They buy a hot jacket potato and a canned drink to have on their way home.

a) How much would this cost to make at home?

b) How much would it cost to eat in a café?

c) Would they be more likely to eat a proper meal if they waited until they arrived home before eating? Suggest a suitable evening meal for them to eat at home. Say why you have made this choice.

Eating habits have changed considerably during the last century, e.g. shift working and TV viewing at mealtimes.

Try to think of at least five more changes.

In any family there are some general points to consider when planning meals:

● How much money is available for food?
● How much time is available for food preparation?
● Is there someone who may need special meals?
● Is the food nutritionally correct for each member of the family?
● How can the meals be planned to suit different family situations?

Meal planning can be helped by the wise use of convenience foods. When shopping we can make a choice between fresh food, convenience food or a combination of both of these.

Health and Food

Fresh foods are mainly purchased 'as seen' but are not always available. They can be expensive and will go bad if not preserved.

Convenience foods have been partly or completely prepared or processed and packaged by a food manufacturer. Most are ready to eat or require very little preparation e.g.

TINS – baked beans
FROZEN – oven chips
DRIED – instant desserts
PREPARED – ready-to-eat dishes

1 In which of the ways shown above can the following foods be obtained?

cheesecake   pizza   sausages   soup   peas

2 Make a comparison between one form of convenience food and another, or the homemade version, e.g.

bread mix, frozen bread, homemade bread
tin of soup, packet soup, homemade soup.

Put your results into a table like this:

	Convenience Type 1	Convenience Type 2	Homemade
Cost (including additional ingredients)			
Time needed to make			
Flavour			
Colour			
Texture			
Quantity			
General comments			

3 List some of the advantages of using convenience foods for:

a) a family camping holiday

b) a one-parent family

c) a family living in a remote country area.

Convenience foods are useful but should not totally replace fresh foods. The clever use of convenience foods *with* fresh foods provides us with meals to suit most people's needs.

Enjoyable mealtimes

Meals can be made more interesting if we consider these points:

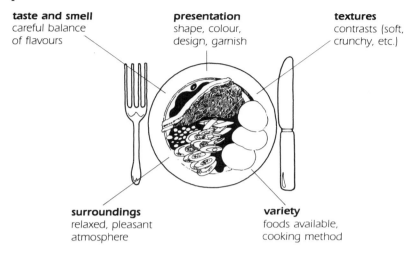

taste and smell
careful balance of flavours

presentation
shape, colour, design, garnish

textures
contrasts (soft, crunchy, etc.)

surroundings
relaxed, pleasant atmosphere

variety
foods available, cooking method

Start good eating habits early to lead to better health in later life. Food should be enjoyable to eat and, if we are sensible, nourishing too. The food we eat not only affects our physical well-being but helps to develop our ideas about what we like and what we don't like – our aesthetic appreciation.

Our need for food changes as we develop and grow older. Each one of us is different which means that we all need different amounts of food each day. This will depend on our

Age   Sex   Health

Work and leisure activity

Climate

Tables of Recommended Daily Allowances (RDA's) such as those in the Manual of Nutrition [HMSO] have been compiled as a guide to:

how much of each nutrient we need, *and*

our daily energy requirements, for optimum health.

These tables are based on averages for the population and do not cover special needs or individual differences as shown in the illustrations on the previous page.

This chart covers some examples of RDA's for a range of ages and activities for both sexes.

Sex/Age Occupation / Nutrient	Boys and Girls 3–5	Boys and Girls 7–9	Boys 12–15	Girls 12–15	Men 35–65 yrs Sedentary	Men 35–65 yrs Very Active	Women 18–55 yrs Most Occupations	Women 18–55 yrs Very Active
Protein	40 g	53 g	70 g	58 g	68 g	90 g	55 g	63 g
Fat and Carbohydrates	Our need for fats and carbohydrates is connected to our need for energy so food tables do not usually include specific recommended amounts. Page 102 indicates how the balance of energy-producing foods is changing towards an increase in starches and a decrease in sugars and fats. For example, adults should try to eat at least 30 g fibre a day and not more than 80 g fat.							
Vitamin C	20 mg	20 mg	25 mg	25 mg	30 mg	30 mg	30 mg	30 mg
Calcium	500 mg	500 mg	700 mg	700 mg	500 mg	500 mg	500 mg	500 mg
Iron	8 mg	10 mg	14 mg	14 mg	10 mg	10 mg	12 mg	12 mg
Energy Intake or Requirements	1600 Kcal or 6.7 MJ	2100 / 8.8	2800 / 11.7	2300 / 9.6	2600 / 10.9	3600 / 15.1	2200 / 9.2	2500 / 10.5

Look at these figures for nutrition in a large burger, a portion of French fries and a milk shake.

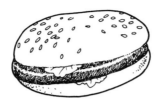

Energy = 550 Kcal
Carbohydrate = 50g
Fat = 30g
Protein = 25g

FRENCH FRIES

Energy = 280 Kcal
Carbohydrate = 35g
Fat = 15g
Protein = 4g

MILK SHAKE

Energy = 375 Kcal
Carbohydrate = 60g
Fat = 10g
Protein = 10g

1 Approximately how much more protein would you need to eat during the rest of the day if this was your meal at midday?

2 What is the total energy value of this meal?

3 What is the approximate percentage of the day's energy intake provided.

4 Suggest reasons why this is a high energy meal.

5 Plan the rest of the day's meals. Think about the dietary guidelines mentioned on p. 102.

FAMILY MEALS

The infant needs

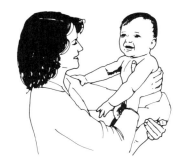

- breast milk if possible for the first four months
- solid foods introduced gradually
- plenty of boiled water
- few sweetened drinks
- suitable foods without too much salt, sugar, fat or additives.

1 Find out what is meant by 'weaning' and suggest at least four suitable foods to start mixed feeding.

2 Look at a selection of commercial baby foods. What does this symbol on the label mean? Why is it important?

3 Your neighbour's young child shows a dislike for milk. How can milk be included in his diet in an interesting and enjoyable way?

The young schoolchild needs

- enough protein for rapid growth
- gradual introduction of a wide variety of foods
- small portions, avoiding snacks between meals
- regular meals
- attractively served food
- sufficient food to provide the energy for constant activity.

1 David spends his school dinner money on his way to school on crisps and sweets. What problems do you think this might cause David? How can his family help him to eat more sensibly?

A First Home Economics Course

2 You are going to look after your 7-year-old cousin after school until bedtime. What would you need to add to the foods shown below to make an interesting evening meal for yourselves?

The teenager needs

- a variety of energy-giving foods for an active and growing body
- a good supply of vitamins and minerals, especially calcium and iron
- common sense when choosing meals, avoiding too much 'junk' food
- to avoid excess carbo-hydrate and fat at the expense of protein
- plenty of sleep and exercise as well as a sound diet
- a diet suitable for adolescent development.

Remember, bad habits are hard to change!

?? PROBLEM PAGE ??
Dear Aunty May,
    My mum thinks that I should have a hot school dinner every day. How can I persuade her that packed lunches are O.K.?
        Jennifer.
PS. I am plump and tend to eat too much.

Dear Jennifer,

May
Aunty May

1 How would you reply to Jennifer, giving some useful suggestions for unusual packed meals?

2. Some school cafeterias are using a traffic-light colour coding system for the foods on their menu.

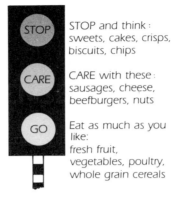

STOP and think: sweets, cakes, crisps, biscuits, chips

CARE with these: sausages, cheese, beefburgers, nuts

Eat as much as you like:
fresh fruit,
vegetables, poultry,
whole grain cereals

a) Do you think this would work in your school to encourage teenagers to eat healthier foods?

b) Which foods in your school cafeteria would fit into each colour code?

As we grow older, the amount of food needed for the body to work normally depends upon:

- the general health of the individual
- the amount of activity in work and leisure
- the size of the body (men generally have a larger frame than women)

The adult needs

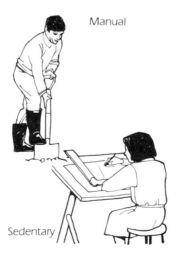

Manual

Sedentary

- to continue with the sound nutritional habits already learned
- a steady intake of all the nutrients needed for the adult lifestyle.
- a manual worker will need a higher energy intake than a sedentary worker. A sedentary worker will need fresh fruit and vegetables, and wholegrain products to aid the digestion (compensating for less activity).
- a varied and interesting diet allowing for occasional treats when rules can be broken.
- to care about diet and health.

activity

Try to discover how ethnic groups living in this country have adapted their traditional eating patterns and food customs.

A First Home Economics Course

Special consideration will need to be given to planning meals for the following groups of people to make sure that their nutritional requirements are adequately met:

expectant mothers
the elderly
invalids and convalescents
vegetarians.

The expectant mother needs

- special medical care to check on normal progress and weight gain
- a good supply of protein, vitamins and minerals – especially iron, for the development of the foetus
- gentle exercise
- to avoid strongly flavoured foods, smoking, alcohol and drugs
- to take advantage of free dental care, prescriptions and free milk, and vitamin supplements if on a low income.

1 'Eating for two' during pregnancy is not to be recommended. Why not?

2 If a mother is breast feeding her new born baby, she must take care with her own diet to produce nourishing milk. Which foods should she eat which include plenty of the required body building nutrients and which foods should she avoid?

The elderly need

- to cut down on fat and carbohydrate as elderly people use less energy
- extra calcium, vitamins D, B, and iron
- smaller meals but still of a good quality
- fibre-rich foods to avoid digestive problems such as constipation
- help from others in times of difficulty.

1 Sometimes elderly people find themselves living alone and are tempted to neglect their diet. How could the following problems be overcome?

a) eating alone

b) cooking in small quantities

c) buying in small quantities

d) lower income

Plan some interesting meals for one.

2 The community in some areas helps the elderly by providing meals-on-wheels, luncheon clubs, etc. What types of voluntary or statutory help for the elderly are available in your area?

Invalids and convalescents need

- plenty of refreshing and nourishing drinks, if permitted
- light, easily digested fresh foods which are rich in protein, vitamins and minerals to speed recovery
- small meals which are hygienically prepared and attractive, served at regular intervals
- to avoid foods which are fried, highly seasoned, rich and stodgy
- a pleasant, caring atmosphere in which to recover.

THE DOCTOR'S INSTRUCTIONS SHOULD ALWAYS BE FOLLOWED.

1 Your family is helping to look after an elderly relative recovering from a serious operation. Plan a day's menu and describe how to serve one of the meals attractively on a tray.

A First Home Economics Course

2 Find out more about which foods could be served during the three main stages of illness:

a) during a fever, at the beginning

b) when the fever begins to break, on the road to recovery

c) in convalescence, heading towards full recovery.

Explain why the type of diet you suggest is different in each case.

Vegetarians need

Vegans

Lacto-vegetarians

- to ensure that an adequate supply of essential nutrients is provided by eating a variety of foods
- to include extra amounts of crisp, fresh and varied fruit and vegetables and whole-grain products
- to supplement their diet sometimes with extra vitamins and minerals (particularly vegans)
- to season food carefully, making use of herbs and spices.

activity

1 Why do people choose to be vegetarians?

2 What are the two main types of vegetarian? Explain the differences between them.

3 Imagine you have invited a lacto-vegetarian friend to your home for an evening meal. Look in some recipe books for ideas and then list some suitable dishes, bearing in mind cost, time to make, and the special foods required.

4 Try to find out what a macrobiotic diet is.

Modified diets are often used to treat illness or prevent future ill health. These medically planned diets are best prescribed by the doctor with advice from qualified dieticians. There are also organisations concerned with particular diets which might be able to offer helpful information, leaflets and recipes, e.g. The Coeliac Society of Great Britain and Northern Ireland.

Examples of modified diets include:

restricted salt   high or low fibre
gluten-free   sugar-free
high or low protein   low or modified fat
milk-free

Nowadays, there is such a wide variety of foods available that following such a diet can be easy, enjoyable and fitted into the family meal plan.

Those concerned with preparing or implementing the diet should be well-informed about the 'dos' and 'don'ts' and should use their common sense.

BUYING AND STORAGE

The money we spend on food must be balanced carefully with other family expenses. Between 25 and 35 per cent of the family's total income is spent on food, but more may be spent by large or low-income families.

Shopping tends to be done less frequently than in the past, with people using supermarkets or hypermarkets to buy food weekly or even monthly instead of daily. Some of the reasons for this are:

- over 60 per cent of food consumed is sold through supermarkets at competitive prices.
- convenience foods which have been processed and packaged to save time and effort will store for a longer time.
- bulk buying can be convenient and cheap if you have sufficient storage space and money.
- most families have a fridge and many have a freezer which means that perishable foods do not have to be purchased daily.

1   Draw a map of a shopping precinct indicating the main types of shop. Give four reasons for the increasing popularity of shopping precincts.

2　List the advantages and disadvantages of shopping at each of the types of shop shown above for these groups of people:

　　a) an elderly couple on a retirement pension

　　b) a student living in a flat with three others, away from home

　　c) a family with two pre-school children.

3　How do you decide where to do your shopping? Look for shops which display:
　　a) cleanliness
　　b) efficiency
　　c) helpfulness
　　d) clear and competitive prices
　　e) a quick turnover of stock
　　f) a good range of products and sizes

　　Are there any other factors which might influence your choice of shop?

4　Copy this table into your notebook. Make a list of your local food shops, assessing each one on the points listed above. Award a score of:

　　*** = very good
　　** = quite good
　　* = slightly below average
　　P = poor

Example:

Food shop	Assessment	Reasons
J. Super-market	***	b), d), e), f)

5　Government Food Hygiene Regulations control all aspects of food handling. Make a list of ten points which shop keepers and assistants should follow to maintain a good standard of hygiene e.g. do not smoke when handling and preparing food.

How do you decide what to buy?

These all lead to impulse buying:

Special offers	No shopping list	TV advertising	Money-off coupons

Try not to buy on impulse with little thought for the other items you need. This will quickly use up your food budget and may cause shortages in other areas of family expense.

Follow these simple guidelines to help the money to be spent wisely:

- Plan ahead and make a shopping list (this will also save time).
- Know how much money to spend.
- Look for competitive prices, taking advantage of special offers only if you need those items.
- Compare the weight and price of different brands.
- Choose good quality food that is good value for money, particularly fruit and vegetables when they are in season.
- Look at the 'sell-by' date so that it can be stored before use if necessary and not wasted.
- Do not buy more than you need unless the food can be used up later or stored safely.
- Buying in bulk needs – extra care about storage, e.g. freezer
  - extra money but will save money in the long term
  - extra time for picking or shopping but will save time overall.
- Buy special treats only after you have bought the essential shopping.

Some examples of bulk buying.

M.R. BUTCHER	Pick Your Own	FROZEN FOODS
MEAT PACKS AT SPECIAL PRICES: 5 kg pork chops 5 kg lean mince Whole Gammon	Strawberries Raspberries Potatoes Sweetcorn All fresh Keen prices	BULK-BUY PACKS 2 lts ICE-CREAM 5 kg GARDEN PEAS COD FILLET

1 Find out the prices of some bulk purchase foods and compare them with standard packs e.g. potatoes, minced beef, ice-creams, etc. Is the saving worthwhile?

2 Give some disadvantages of bulk buying.

Many foods only remain edible for a short time under normal conditions in our homes. If perishable foods are not stored correctly they will go bad. Ripening is a natural process caused by enzyme action (see Glossary p. 173). This process of decay is caused by micro-organisms. These micro-organisms include yeasts, moulds and bacteria which, although invisible, are always around us.

How micro-organisms are spread:

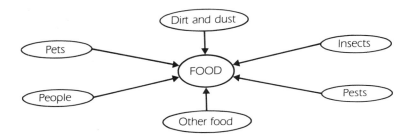

Keeping food COOL, CLEAN and COVERED will reduce the risk of infection from eating unsafe food.

Some foods are more 'at risk' than others and need careful storage and handling, e.g. meat and meat products, fish, milk and cream, eggs, and dishes containing these foods.

Rules for storing food:

- Cool leftover food quickly and use within 24 hours.
- Store foods correctly, according to their type.
- Take note of the keeping time on the label.
- Do not refreeze thawed food.
- Use up old stocks of food before opening new ones.
- Keep all storage places and storage containers clean.

Modern houses have little room for a traditional larder and storage space is often provided by cupboards and a refrigerator.

Larders and cupboards must be ventilated, e.g. by a grill or air-brick.

Ways of storing food

Dry foods
+12 °C

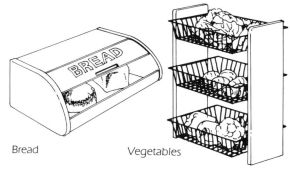

Semi-perishable
foods 6° to 12 °C

Bread   Vegetables

Freezer

Ready-frozen foods
−18 °C

Fridge

Perishable foods
+6 °C
e.g. eggs, cheese,
milk, meat

activity

1 Find out what this star marking system means on frozen
foods and on the ice box.

One   *
Two   **
Three   ***

A First Home Economics Course

2 *Matching game* – match the foods with the correct method of storage:

Food	A	B	C	D	E
Storage					

 A

 B

 C

 D

 E

 1

 2

 3 Crisper drawer

4 Larder

5

CONSUMER INFORMATION

Every label tells a story . . . or does it?

Can you imagine shopping for our groceries if all tins and packets were not clearly labelled?

Packaging is now part of everyday life and most people take it for granted. A package contains and preserves the contents so that they can be handled, distributed, sold and stored.

Most manufacturers advertise their products widely hoping that they will have instant appeal to the consumer.

A label should:

- inform the customer what the product is and the quantity.
- state all the ingredients used.
- be attractive.
- be clear and easily understood.

In your opinion, do these labels fulfil what the points listed above suggest?

A First Home Economics Course

Labels must not be misleading – either unintentionally or deliberately. There are Food Labelling Regulations which guide and guard the shopper. These are now in line with the EEC customer protection programme.

In general, prepacked foods must have labels which show:

Name of the food and description →

Net weight →

Date mark →

COOKING INSTRUCTIONS–
ROCK CAKES
1. Pre-heat oven to 220°C, 425°F, Gas Mark 7.
2. Lightly grease baking sheet.
3. Empty contents of packet into mixing bowl and rub in 50 gram (2 oz) of butter or margarine until mixture resembles fine breadcrumbs.
4. Mix in 50 gram (2 oz) dried fruit.
5. Add one beaten egg (size 3) and one tablespoon of water and mix to form a stiff dough.
6. Using a teaspoon, place 12 rough heaps onto the baking sheet and bake at the top of the oven for approximately 15 minutes until golden.
Makes 12 cakes.

RECIPE SUGGESTIONS
Chocolate Chip Buns
Follow instructions as above replacing the dried fruit with 50 gram (2 oz) chocolate drops for cooking.
Coconut and Cherry Pyramids
Follow instructions as above replacing the dried fruit with 50 gram (2 oz) desiccated coconut and 50 gram (2 oz) chopped glace cherries.
Roll the mixture into 12 balls and pinch on top into rough pyramid shapes.

← Instructions for use, including any additional ingredients needed for some foods

Ingredients listed in order of quantity near to the name of the product or in a box →

Bar code for stock control and pricing →

Name and address of manufacturer and place or origin if necessary →

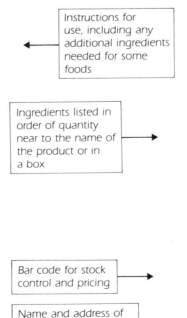

ROCK CAKE BASE MIX
add butter, egg and dried fruit

Ingredients: Wheat flour, Sugar, Raising agents: Acid sodium aluminium phosphate, Sodium bicarbonate; Flavouring

J Sainsbury plc Stamford Street London SE1 9LL

The Trading Standards Department, usually based at the Town Hall, is responsible for enforcing the law on food labelling. Complaints about a food can also be dealt with through it or the Local Authority's Environmental Health Department.

A few manufacturers are now including nutritional information on their own brand's packs. e.g. Birdseye, and they may also include it in free leaflets, e.g. 'A Tesco Guide to Healthy Eating' which explains that their aim is to make 'healthy eating an ordinary, everyday, routine event'.

Tesco have added these and other logos to their own labels to make it easier for customers to choose a selection of healthier foods:

1 Do you think this nutritional information on labels is of use to the average consumer?

2 Ask these simple questions of some of your friends, family and neighbours:

a) If you look at labels when you buy food, what is the information you are searching for?

b) Do you think about the nutritional value of a food when you buy it?

c) Would you find it beneficial if other manufacturers used Tesco's labelling scheme?

3 *Evaluation* – from the answers you have been given, do you think that more people are taking notice of how certain foods can affect their health?

What is your opinion?

A First Home Economics Course

4 Imagine you are in charge of launching a new product on to the market. Say what this product is and how you would plan your campaign. Design the label for the package.

FOOD ADDITIVES

Manufactured foods often contain certain substances which will:

- help to maintain the nutritional quality of the food
- improve its appearance, flavour, colour or texture
- help in the processing and preparation of the food
- preserve the food from decay.

These substances are called **additives.**

Additives are not new, many of them have been in use for a long time. Sugar and salt are the commonest food additives and are eaten in the largest quantities. Others may be added by manufacturers, but the use of additives is strictly controlled by the **1984 Food Act**.

Category	Use	Examples
Preservatives	Protect food against spoilage; increase shelf life	E200 E252
Antioxidants	Stop rancidity in fatty foods and protect fat soluble vitamins	E300 E322
Emulsifiers and Stabilisers	Mix foods or stop them from separating	E410 E414
Colours	Make food more colourful, especially after processing	E102 E150

E numbers have been approved by the European Economic Community as safe and permissible additives. In the UK there are other permitted categories such as flavour enhancers and sweeteners, and several more are under consideration for control.

A few people, particularly children, may develop allergic reactions to some of the chemicals in food.

It is important to remember that lack of food hygiene is more likely to make you ill than any of the additives currently allowed in foods.

1 Margarine has vitamins A and D added to it by law during manufacture. Which other foods have substances added:

a) by law during manufacture?

b) voluntarily by the manufacturers as a selling point?

2 Within your group bring a selection of food labels from packets or tins, frozen and fresh foods, e.g.:
loaf of bread, packet of instant mousse, frozen peas, tinned milk pudding, coffee whitener.
List these in your notebook as headings.

a) Under each heading list the ingredients as shown on the label.

b) Against each ingredient state whether it is a natural ingredient or an additive. If possible, give the purpose of the additive.

c) Is any product a purely natural one?

Food plays an important part in our plans for healthy living. It can make the difference between feeling fit and well or always being 'one degree under'.

A First Home Economics Course

Section Four

Health and Dress

FASHION

Clothes have been likened to a 'second skin'.

We have seen that a healthy skin can make us more attractive whereas we appear less good looking if it is uncared for, dirty and dull. Although different in some respects, many of the properties of skin and clothes are the same.

Skin

Skin/Clothing

Clothing

- Is flexible and allows us mobility
- Shows signs of wear with age
- Keeps in the heat when we are cold but lets it out when we are hot
- Acts as a barrier against sun, wind, rain and germs
- Protects our organs and skeleton
- Shows our feelings
- Shows our state of health
- Allows us to be physically attractive

- Keeps in body fluids
- Heals itself after wounds and cuts
- Grows and replaces dead tissues
- Allows us to feel pain, textures and temperature
- Helps to make vitamin D using sunlight

- Should be right for the time of day and occasion
- Should suit your colouring and looks
- can reflect your personality

Do you agree that your clothes act like a second skin?

Presenting an attractive appearance gives us confidence in ourselves and contributes to our success in today's society. We already know that caring for ourselves is important in our aim to live as healthy a life as possible. We also need to think about our presentation not only from the inside but also from the outside. Having a good sense of dress allows us to express ourselves while experimenting in the world of fashion.

HISTORY

For thousands of years humans have made use of the different types of fabric for covering their bodies and to make shelters. Some of the earliest materials used were the skins and furs of animals. They provided warmth, protection and shelter from the elements outside.

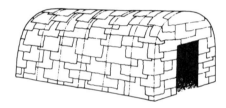

A longhouse: animal skins and bark over a wooden frame

A tepee: decorated hide stretched over poles

Primitive homes in North America

Reeds and grasses were also used, particularly for roofing. To do this, the strands had to be twisted around each other. This method led to the production of the first woven fabrics.

Tent of carved poles supporting
woven reed and grass mats
(Somalia)

Woven reed house
(Republic of Niger)

Primitive homes in Africa

Since these early beginnings, a greater interest in personal
appearance and fashion has developed out of the simple
necessity to wear clothes. A study of costume throughout
each historical period shows how politics, royalty, wars and
economic conditions influence dress.

Features such as frills, types of collar and sleeves, different
hem-lines, and many basic shapes have been in and out of
fashion several times. This constant swing in fashion also
applies to the use of accessories, jewellery, hats, hairstyles
and make-up.

Ladies' dress of the 1900s
– a very graceful
and feminine
style

The 'swinging sixties'
– styled to suit
the 'swinging' image

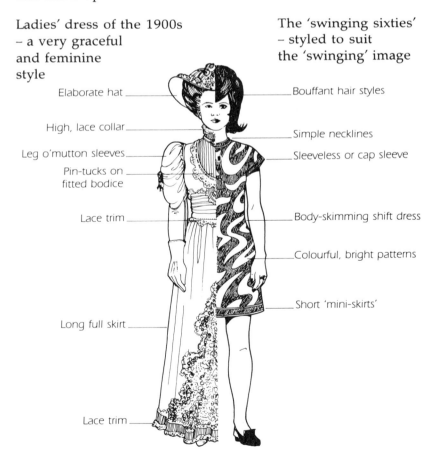

Elaborate hat

High, lace collar

Leg o'mutton sleeves

Pin-tucks on
fitted bodice

Lace trim

Long full skirt

Lace trim

Bouffant hair styles

Simple necklines

Sleeveless or cap sleeve

Body-skimming shift dress

Colourful, bright patterns

Short 'mini-skirts'

These illustrations show examples of changes in style and design for both men's and women's clothing.

Nobleman (1105)

Lady (1130)

The styles of the Norman period (eleventh and twelfth centuries) were dignified and simple.

Twelfth-century dress

Princess (1546)
Brocade gown
Girdle and neckline jewelled
Velvet false sleeves with slashes
French hood

The fifteenth century saw frequent changes in costume and, owing to the wars of this time, French styles influenced English clothing. The reign of Henry VIII in the sixteenth century was a period of extravagant dress. Fabrics were costly and richly trimmed, often with fur or jewels.

Henry VIII (1536)
Gold cloth gown with fur
Doublet
Jerkin
Slashed sleeves
Slashed shoes
Hose

Sixteenth-century dress

In the early twentieth century, the suffragette movement began to challenge the role of women in society. The two world wars completed the revolution in dress, particularly for women. More women were involved in civilian work outside the home, and in the Women's Services.

WAAF Flight Officer 1941
Air Force blue
barathea uniform

Sub-lieutenant
Royal Navy 1939–41

1940s' Services dress

1948
Crêpe dress with
dolman sleeve

The 'New Look' from Dior combined practicality with femininity. Clothes for men had simple, clear-cut lines.

1948
Single-breasted
lounge suit
Black leather shoes

The 'New Look'

Some features of clothes worn today have their origins in different countries. The ones illustrated on p. 132 clearly show their ethnic background.

 activity

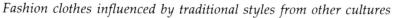

Fashion clothes influenced by traditional styles from other cultures

These illustrations show the style of clothes worn by wealthy people in the early Victorian period (about 1850).

1842–4
Black silk top hat
Tail coat with black velvet collar
Black silk neckcloth
Cane
Light grey trousers
Black boots

1847–8
Green silk and cotton day dress
Deep lavender silk mantelet
Lavender silk bonnet

1   Work in groups to create a collage of figures illustrating family life in Victorian times for rich or poor people. You may like to 'dress' your figures using scraps of suitable materials and glue. A visit to the historical section of your library will help you to understand more about the clothes people wore and their life style.

Try to imagine what it would be like to live at this time.

Label your figures to show such points as colour, fabric, transport, comfort, care of garments, leisure activities and accessories.

2 Look at the families you have created.
Why do you think that there is such a contrast between the rich and the poor?

3 Alternatively, you could do a similar study for any other period in history in which you may have particular interest, e.g. the 1940s.

Today we live in a whirl of constantly changing fashion which can be so extreme at times that it is hard for the ordinary person to be in fashion all of the time. Few of us could afford to change our entire wardrobe at regular intervals simply to be fashionable. The best we can often do is to:

- follow the trend of fashion created by fashion designers and manufacturers
- choose styles and adapt them to suit ourselves
- avoid being ruled by the whims of the fashion world.

Try to remember that the clothes you see in fashion magazines and on people in the public eye like pop stars may not necessarily look very good on you.

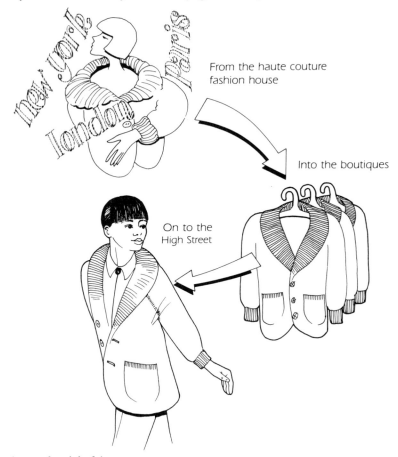

From the haute couture fashion house

Into the boutiques

On to the High Street

The path of fashion

PERSONALITY

Clothes are still worn today, as they were many years ago, because of our basic need for protection. However, there are now many more reasons for wearing clothes:

- to enhance our way of life, for comfort and convenience
- to express our own personality and to display our character to others.

You may not think that it matters what other people see you wearing, but remember that the way you dress will always say something about you to other people.

These are some of the messages sent to other people by the way you dress:

CLOTHES

can be used to emphasise our good points and disguise the bad ones.

can indicate our status in society and our financial status.

may illustrate particular religious beliefs or pro-fessional status.

help our whole body to reflect our personality.

are suitable for our climate and the era in which we live.

can show some connection with tradition or culture.

show our age, school, interests.

Do you always send the right messages?

discussion area

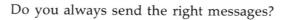

Consider the clothes you are now wearing. What other messages might your clothes pass on to others? Why do you think we wear different clothes for different occasions?

Wearing clothes which are suited to us shows good dress sense.

What does this mean?

First of all, look at yourself in a mirror.

- How do you see yourself?
- How does the world see you?

The world sees us as we really are

How we see ourselves is influenced by what we want to see

If you find it difficult to view yourself in a mirror as you really are, try looking at other people and see what you notice about them.

- What are their good points and bad points? e.g. strong, square shoulders; well-proportioned figure; big feet; too thin etc.
- Do they draw attention to their good points and disguise their bad ones?
- How do you think their personality is reflected in the way they dress?

To create the right appearance for yourself, you need to know yourself. Copy out the following self-analysis chart and perhaps stick a recent photograph of yourself in your notebook which you could analyse.

Underline the word(s) applicable to you or put in your own choice.

As I see myself:

a) My hair is (straight, wavy, tightly curled) and my complexion is (dark, sallow, fair).

b) The shape of my face is (oval, round, square, oblong, triangular).

c) My neck is (long, thin, short, fat, average).

d) My outline is (slim, tall, plump, short, average, well-built).

e) I have an (upright, slouching) posture.

f) My body measurements are (well-proportioned, not well-proportioned).

g) I am usually (quiet, shy, subdued, light-hearted, a show-off, bubbly).

h) My favourite colours are . . . (choose three)

i) I prefer to wear (plain, simple, casual, special occasion, flamboyant, fussy) clothes.

My favourite outfit is . . .

because . . .

There are a number of ways of achieving an attractive appearance, but the careful selection of **colour**, **style** and **fabric** is the key to success.

COLOUR

This needs to be chosen with care. Think about the effect it will have on your total look, your figure shape, your personality and the shape of the garments that you wear.

Copy this colour wheel into your notebook. Use crayons or felt tips to colour in the various sections as described below.

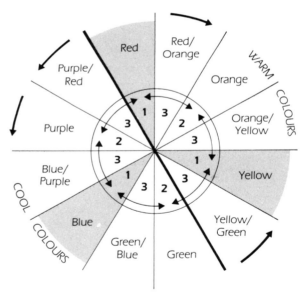

a) Colour in the three primary sections (red, yellow and blue).

b) Blend red and yellow for the orange section, yellow and blue for the green section, blue and red for the purple section.

c) You can now combine these colours to make the six sections labelled '3'.

Do you prefer the warm or the cool colours or the primary colours or shades?

Colours can be thought of as having a personality. The colour wheel is a guide to this, e.g. what does the colour red convey to you?

This information helps us to use colour to create an attractive appearance. The best colours for *you* are those which go with the colour of your eyes, hair and skin. A clever use of colour can play tricks with your appearance.

Here is some simple advice about using colour:

i) Do not be afraid to use colour – be adventurous.

ii) Choose a shade of the colours in fashion to suit you, even if only buying an accessory.

iii) Look at your existing clothes before buying a 'new' colour, to see if they will combine.

iv) An assortment of colours can be fashionable but it is expensive to keep up to date all of the time.

v) Sometimes a splash of colour is sufficient to give new interest to a dull appearance.

Look at your self-analysis chart. Compare your comments with this chart. Do you consider that you use colour to your advantage? Copy the chart into your notebook and then fill in examples of suitable colours in the third column:

Complete this column:

Personal details	General colour description	Examples of actual colours
Fair complexions	Most colours	
Dark hair/ sallow skin	Bright, vivid colours	
High complex- ions/auburn hair	Cool colours	
To look larger	Pale colours	
To look slimmer	Dark colours	
For a 'warm' effect	Red, yellow, orange are vibrant	
For a 'cool' effect	Blues and greens are restful	

STYLE

Style lines and features can be used to deceive the eye and to alter the way we look.

Some features can be used to develop a pleasing appearance, e.g.

- patterns on a fabric
- garment construction lines
- neck-lines, hem-lines, sleeves, etc.

However, the result can be confused if not enough thought is given to the effect that these optical illusions create.

1 Look at these groups of lines and the different effects they create. All of them can be seen in the clothes we wear. By using this information you can make yourself look taller and thinner or shorter and wider.

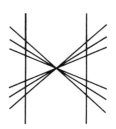

Here the vertical lines seem to curve but they are actually straight.

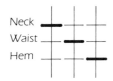

The eye can be drawn to focal points at neck, waist or hem level, allowing faults to be minimised and good points to be emphasised.

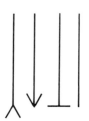

These lines are exactly the same length, but the use of horizontal and diagonal lines makes them appear different lengths.

You can choose a basic shape that you think suits you best. Here are some examples.

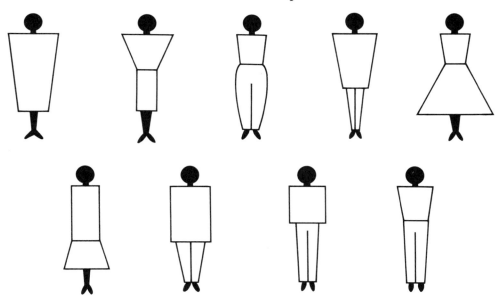

2   Have a look at your personal analysis (pp. 135–6). Do the clothes you wear achieve the right effect for your figure type?

Focus on design

a)   *PAM* – is an attractive girl with a pretty face and thick, shiny hair. She worries about being too thin.

     Design and sketch some outfits which would help to emphasise her good features.

b)   *DAVE* – has just bought a new leather jacket. He wants to present a 'street-wise' fashion image, without very much further expense.

     Design a range of casuals to complement his choice of basic garment.

FABRIC

This also has the ability to affect our appearance. The texture must be suitable for the design, e.g. bulky material does not gather satisfactorily.

Textures can:

- reflect or absorb light – Shiny fabrics, e.g. satin, appear to increase your size. Non-shiny fabrics are more flattering to a large figure.

- be rough, smooth or fluffy – Rough textures suit thin people better than larger people because they tend to increase size.

- be stiff, soft or clinging – Stiff fabrics hide the outline of the figure but often make a heavy body larger. Fabrics which drape well, particularly clinging ones, can be attractive on a slim figure but over-emphasise a not so well-proportioned figure.

Try to find some interesting textures of fabrics, e.g. a smooth velvet or a rough tweed. Stick them into your notebook.

What effect will each one have on:

1 a plump figure which is
   a) tall   b) short

2 a slim figure which is
   a) tall   b) short?

As well as texture the quality of the fabric is important. Good-quality fabric, although often expensive, will make garments which wear well and retain their shape. Garments made of poorer quality material can soon look shoddy, may stretch during wear or shrink when washed. A poor choice of colour, style and fabric results in a badly dressed appearance.

FASHION BUYING

There are several points which should be thought about before you go shopping, during your shopping expedition and after you have made your choice.

A First Home Economics Course

- **before you go shopping**

Know how much you want to spend and what you want to buy.

Before you discard any clothing ask yourself if it could be repaired or cleaned and still be worn.

How would my new clothes and accessories add interest to my old ones?

Good quality and fashionable clothes can be sold, e.g. through a dress agency.

Older, not so fashionable clothes can be given to charity shops or jumble sales to help to raise money for good causes.

How will my present outfits blend with this year's fashion colours?

- **during your shopping expedition**

Decide which type of shops you want to look at.

Have some idea of what you are buying for – season, long-lasting, easy to wash, etc.

Sales assistants can be helpful but do not let them be too persuasive. Try the clothes on if possible.

Shop when you feel like it – being tired and unwell may affect your judgement.

Try not to overspend, although good quality is worth saving up for.

Does the latest fashion have the right effect on your personality?

Avoid buying on impulse or in desperation.

Look at the information on the labels.

- **after shopping**

Keep receipts as proof of purchase if goods need to be exchanged.

Beware – sales bargains may not be bargains if you are never going to wear them.

Treat your clothes with care – keep them clean and in good repair.

You should return faulty goods for an exchange or refund as soon as possible.

Goods must be as they are stated to be, e.g. waterproof, leather. Know your consumer rights.

A few money saving ideas:

- Everybody buys a few 'fun' clothes occasionally, but it is unlikely that they will be fashionable for very long so it is not wise to spend a lot of money on them.
- Buying clothes reduced in sales, as 'seconds', from market stalls or second-hand can spin out your clothing allowance.
- Could you make some of your clothes? Some designs are easy and cheap to make and it is an interesting and useful way of spending your leisure time.

ACCESSORIES

To complete the way we look we should always consider the right choice of underwear, accessories, hairstyle and make-up. It is no use being well-dressed on the outside if your underwear is dirty and smelly, uncomfortable, or unsuitable for your outfit. The same can be said for any accessories you want to add such as shoes, hat, scarf, gloves, belt, bag, tie and jewellery.

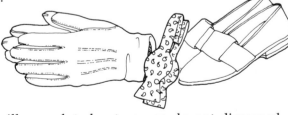

Your choice will say a lot about you so do not disregard their importance. A change of accessories will transform an outfit. This may be more economical than buying a complete new outfit for your next special occasion. Beware of over-

doing it, particularly with the use of jewellery. In your choice of accessories consider your age, your shape, the garments they are to be worn with and the occasion.

> You, your clothes AND your accessories should look as if they are going to the same occasion or place!

On p. 139 you designed some clothes for Pam and Dave. Now choose the accessories they would add to those outfits for particular occasions such as:

a) staying with a friend for the weekend, which will include a visit to the theatre.

b) going to a special disco at the Youth Club where he/she hopes to make an impression on a new girl/boy friend.

or make up some of your own situations.

Having the right *hairstyle* will add to your confidence. Use the following points to choose the right style for you:

- Hair can be styled to add width or length to the face.
- Do not be too easily influenced by your favourite pop star's styling – it may not suit you.
- Get the advice of your friend or your parents before taking the plunge with a new style.
- Have it restyled professionally.

In recent years, boys and girls, men and women have started to have a unisex approach to dress. They wear each other's style of clothing and accessories, such as handbags, hats, make-up, jewellery and so on.

discussion area

What are your views on this unisex approach to dress? Discuss your views on this subject within your group.

The use of a hand-bag by men on the Continent is an accepted sight. Why are men so wary of using handbags in this country?

Make-up

This can be used to create different effects depending on the occasion for which it is used, how it is applied and the type and quantity of make-up used.

Stage make-up, for example, is used for many dramatic looks, e.g. a young person can be made to look very old, and artificial wounds and scars distort an actor's face. Have you seen a play at school, on TV, or at a theatre recently where you have noticed the clever make-up?

1 Find pictures of some of your favourite pop stars. Do they wear make-up? Write down why you think they do. Is it their good looks which attracts you to them?

2 Trace these silhouettes into your notebook and create some new hairstyles which you like. They can easily be adapted to a male or female form. Now experiment with the application of make-up on the same profiles using coloured crayons.

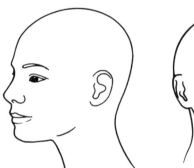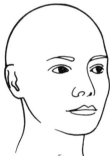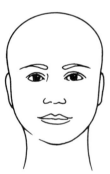

DRESS SENSE

Modern-day living goes along at a fairly rapid pace. For many people the day begins with a journey, in all weathers, to school, office or factory. It may be many hours before we can return home to change or freshen up. All this is very demanding on the clothes we wear. We need to show good sense in choosing clothes which:

- suit the purpose and the occasion
- will remain looking good for many hours
- let us feel physically comfortable during the day
- protect us from the weather

A First Home Economics Course

- allow us to feel at ease mentally and give a boost to our self-confidence
- require the minimum amount of time for laundering and repair.

Have you ever been to a party very smartly dressed and found everyone else in jeans and tee-shirt? We should be able to apply our dress sense to modern-day living so that we can put our clothes on and then forget them. In this way we are promoting healthy living and avoiding stress.

Your combination of life style and dress should give physical comfort and wearability.

Try a quick assessment of your clothing today by answering these questions in your book:

YES   NO   PARTLY

Is it:

a) too hot/too cold?

b) too tight and restricting your movement?

c) suitable for the day's activity i.e. a day at school?

d) very up-to-the-minute in fashion?

e) very creased?

Does it:

f) have several dirty marks and stains?

g) have worn patches, broken seams, or a hem coming down?

h) allow you scope for showing your personality?

i) allow you to feel physically comfortable?

j) give you pleasure to wear it?

Score (Number of marks in brackets)
Questions a), b), d), e), f), g):   Answer Yes (0), No (2), partly (1).
Questions c), h), i), j):   Answer Yes (2), No (0), partly (1).

The higher your mark, the better your dress sense.

TYPES OF FABRIC

The fabrics from which your clothes are made will contribute towards their comfort, hygienic qualities, attractiveness, durability and suitability.

Before the beginning of this century you would only have been able to choose fabrics made from **natural fibres**. The most important ones are:

WOOL ⟶ animal fibres
SILK ⟶

COTTON ⟶ vegetable fibres
LINEN ⟶

Source

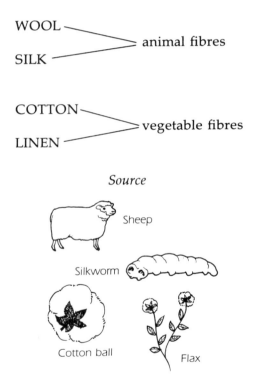

Sheep

Silkworm

Cotton ball   Flax

Other natural fibres less widely used are:

jute and hemp – made into sacks and carpet backing

hair – from goats to make mohair, cashmere, camel hair fabrics; from rabbits to make angora.

Towards the end of the nineteenth century the first **man-made** fibre was produced. It was called artificial silk because it was smooth and shiny like real silk.

We now have two types of man-made fibres:

Source

A REGENERATED FIBRES
e.g. viscose rayon

Cheap plant fibre
such as softwood

Oil

B SYNTHETIC FIBRES
e.g. nylon, acrylic,
polyester, elastomer

Coal

FACTS

- Fleece from a mountain sheep is harsher and more hard-wearing than the softer fleece of the downland sheep.
- Cashmere makes beautifully soft fabrics and is the most expensive of the woollen yarns.
- A silk worm can spin a continuous filament (thread) 1 to 2 km (0.6 to 1.2 miles) in length.
- Silk makes the most expensive fabrics you can buy. It is prized for its sheen, softness and fineness.
- Cotton can be produced more cheaply than wool, much of the harvesting, spinning and weaving is done by machine.
- The softest and better-quality cotton fabrics are produced in the West Indies and Egypt where the tropical climate and wet soil encourages good cotton plants.
- It is the stems of the flax plant which are used to make linen. The outer husk is rotted away and the inner fibres used.
- Linen fibres are very strong and uneven.
- A Frenchman, Chardonett, made the first artificial silk (a regenerated fibre) and it was exhibited at the Paris Exhibition in 1880.
- The first synthetic fibre to be made was nylon, first produced in 1935 by Wallace Hume Carothers.
- Man-made fibres are made as continuous filaments – just as the silkworm produces silk, but the filament is often cut into short lengths and used to imitate natural fibres.

Find out:

1 Which are the major regions of the world for producing natural fibres and fabrics. Obtain map outlines of the UK and the world to stick in your book. Colour in and label these major regions of production.

2 Something about the background history of fibres. Write a paragraph about some of the following:
   a) The treatment of the American slave labour used in the cotton industry during the seventeenth and eighteenth centuries.
   b) The original meaning of the word 'spinster'.
   c) The life of a child worker in an eighteenth-century Lancashire cotton mill.
   d) The traditional knitting of the Scottish Islands.
   e) The effects of synthetic fibres on the Irish linen industry.
   f) The uses of nylon during the Second World War.

FIBRES TO YARNS TO FABRICS

Fibres to yarns

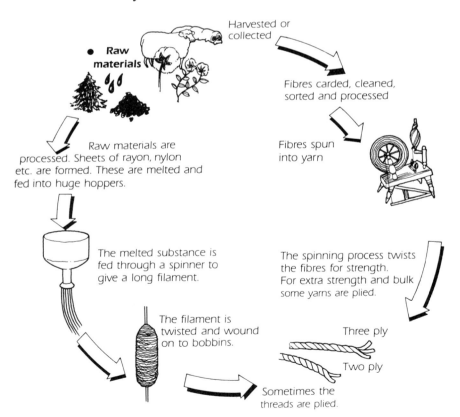

● **Raw materials**

Harvested or collected

Fibres carded, cleaned, sorted and processed

Fibres spun into yarn

Raw materials are processed. Sheets of rayon, nylon etc. are formed. These are melted and fed into huge hoppers.

The melted substance is fed through a spinner to give a long filament.

The spinning process twists the fibres for strength. For extra strength and bulk some yarns are plied.

The filament is twisted and wound on to bobbins.

Three ply

Two ply

Sometimes the threads are plied.

A First Home Economics Course

Yarns to fabrics

The three main ways of making fabric:

Weaving
To weave a fabric a loom is used.
This can be a simple
loom to use at home
or
A large commercial
loom in a factory.

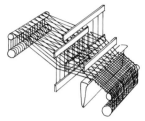 

Knitted fabrics
The yarn forms interlocking loops to produce a
fabric. The simplest is weft-knitted fabric.

Interlock fabric.

Non-woven fabrics such as disposable web fabric.
This is cheap and can be made into underwear,
aprons, dusters, hospital garments. It is very
hygienic as it is thrown away after use.

J. cloth fabric.

From **fibre** to **yarn** to **fabric** can be a simple process or
a very complicated one. The basic processes are shown
above. We have huge factories which turn out thousands of
metres of woven and knitted fabrics, but the basic methods
are simple and *you* can make some fabric from the raw
material and make a completed article – it is not difficult.

Many people find that spinning, weaving and knitting are
fascinating hobbies. It is very relaxing and these activities are
often used as therapy for people under mental stress.

Leisure time activities

Spinning, weaving and knitting skills

To make your own woollen yarn

i) Collect some woollen fleece from the hedges of fields where sheep graze. Clean the fleece.

ii) You will need a *spindle* (**A**). Tie a piece of yarn to the spindle as shown in (**B**).

iii) Blend some of the wool fibres into the end of the length of yarn coming from the top of the spindle.

iv) Spin the spindle clockwise, as the spindle spins it will twist the fibres to make a thread.

v) Keep blending in pieces of fleece and twisting the spindle. As the length of yarn becomes longer twist it round the spindle (**C**).

It takes a lot of practice to learn this skill of spinning, but if you persevere you will soon have a ball of home-spun wool. Use your wool to weave or knit a garment or article.

Shaft of wood

Whorl

A

B

C

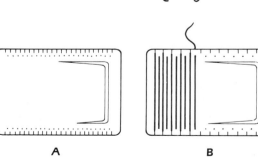
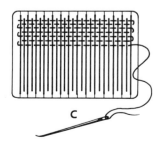

A

B

C

Home-made looms

A First Home Economics Course

The loom on p. 150 is made from a supermarket food tray.

i) The top and bottom edges are strengthened with Sellotape. Notches are cut and holes pierced close together at regular intervals. (**A**)

ii) The warp (down threads) are wound on round the notches and through the holes. (**B**)

iii) The weft (across threads) are threaded through using a long curved bodkin. (**C**)

These squares would make table mats, or join together for larger articles.

A more permanent loom is shown in (**D**). This is made from strips of wood, glued or nailed together.

Nails are then knocked in at regular intervals.

The warp yarn is threaded round the nails. Much larger pieces of fabric can be made on this type of frame loom.

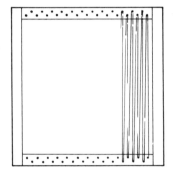

D

Knitting

Casting on

Knit stitch

Purl stitch

Simple garter stitch squares or oblongs will make these:

Blanket

Hat and scarf

Sleeveless sweater

During the spinning and weaving processes different patterns and textures can be introduced, making the fabrics more interesting and useful.

You may have heard of or seen some of the fabrics named below:

Woollen – tweed
jersey
gaberdine
flannel
crêpe

Cotton – denim
twill
corduroy
needlecord
lawn

Silk – taffeta
satin
velvet
shantung
chiffon

Linen – damask
slubbed

Man-made – nylon   Crimplene   rayon
Terylene   Polyester   Tricel
Trevira   Acrilan   Lycra

activity

Make or buy a scrap-book. Make a collection of all the different types of fabric you can find to mount into your scrap-book. Group them under the headings shown above.

COTTON
poplin

Natural fibre
Very soft and smooth
Good colours, fine, strong
Sews and launders well
Use for:-blouses, shirts,
children's and babies'
clothing.

Write some useful information about each piece, for example natural or man-made, cheap or expensive, easily laundered, crease-resistant, which garments it is suitable for.

Experiment with your fabric samples to see if they resist creasing, burn easily, are colour-fast, etc.

Your teacher will help you.

A First Home Economics Course

PROPERTIES AND SPECIAL FINISHES

Fibres have special qualities which make them valuable for making into fabrics for different purposes. These qualities are known as **properties** and include:

absorbency	strength	insulation
coolness	warmth	lustre
resilience	flammability	elasticity
crease-resistance	non-porous	ease of sewing
ease of washing	cost	windproof
water-repellent	feel	texture
drape.		

Use a dictionary to look up any of these words which you do not understand.

All fibres do not have all the properties as you will see from the chart on p. 154. Therefore some fibres are mixed together to give a **blended** fabric – we can then, for instance, combine all the advantages of a man-made fibre mixed with all the advantages of a natural fibre, giving us a very useful fabric.

If you study the chart on the following page you will see that all the natural fibres have a high degree of absorbency and elasticity, and they drape and handle well.

Man-made fibres are generally stong, water-repellent, easy to wash and quite inexpensive.

Here are some examples of common fibre combinations, and the reasons for making them:

- wool and nylon to give strength, absorbency and warmth
- cotton and polyester to give strength, resistance to creasing, absorbency, ease of washing and coolness
- acrylic, wool and polyester for warmth, strength, softness and washability
- nylon and elastomer for stretchability, support and quick drying.

Fibres are also blended to help the fabric to retain dyes more readily, to be set into pleats better and to give special effects of texture and lustre.

discussion area

Why do we think of natural fibres being 'healthier'; especially in hot weather, for babies and young children, for sports wear and for bed clothes.

Fabrics and their properties – at-a-glance chart

	Absorbency	Strength	Insulation	Coolness	Warmth	Lustre	Resilience resists creasing	Flammability resistance	Elasticity	Wind-proof Non-porous	Water-repellent	Feel	Texture drape	Ease of washing	Cost cheapness
Wool	••••	•	•••		•••		•••	••	••			••	••	•	•
Silk	•••	••	•••	•••	••	•••	••	••	••			•••	•••		
Cotton	••••	•••	••	•••	••	•	•	•	••			•••	•••	•••	•••
Linen	••••	••••	••	•••	••	••	•	•				••	••		
Rayon	•••			•	•	•••	•	•				•	•••	•	•••
Synthetics (e.g. nylon)		•••	••		•••	••	•••	••	•••	•••	•••	•	••	••	•••
Acrylic	•	••	••	•	•••		••	••	••	••	••	••	••	••	••
Polyester		•••	••	•	•	••	••	••	••	••	••	••	••	•••	••
Elastomer (elastic materials)		•••	•		••	•	••	•	••	••	•	•	•	••	••

FACTS

Fibres can be blended:

- by spinning the fibres together in a yarn
- by plying two or more yarns of different fibres together
- by weaving different yarns together, using different fibres for warp and weft. This is called a union of fibres.

Different fibres spun together

Wool and nylon yarns plied together

Nylon and woollen yarns woven together.

When making up garments, clothing manufacturers will need to choose suitable fabrics. The properties of the fabrics must suit the purpose of the garment.

A child's dungarees need to be

— Hard-wearing
— Easily washed
— Attractive
— Colour fast
— Stretchy

What fabric properties would these garments need and why?

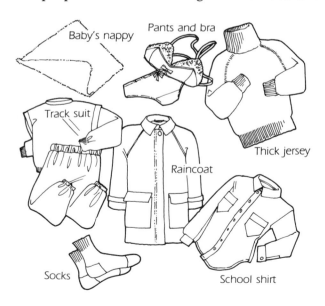

Baby's nappy

Pants and bra

Track suit

Raincoat

Thick jersey

Socks

School shirt

Modern technology has come up with many ways of allowing us to choose clothes which are healthier, safer, more comfortable, look better, wear better and are easier to care for than before.

This has been brought about by the development of special finishes which are applied to the fabrics to improve their normal qualities. Examples are:

For easy care

minimum iron	– a special process or weave to help reduce ironing e.g. Bel-O-Fast
shrink-resistant	– helps to prevent shrinking and allows machine washing e.g. Superwash wool, Rigmel, Sanforised cotton. Some garments are pre-shrunk before wear, e.g. jeans.
permanent creases	– to fix in pleats, trouser creases, etc. e.g. Evaprest, Fixaform.
dye-fast	– a **mordant** is used to fix dye in a fabric. Strong colours often run during washing.

For good looks and wearability

stiffening fabrics	– a process to avoid the need to starch parts such as collars, e.g. **Trubenising.**
stain-resistant/ water-repellant	– reduces the fabric's ability to absorb stains and moisture and oil, e.g. Scotchgard, Zepel.
crease-resistant	– fabrics which crease badly such as linen can have the fibres coated with resin to make them more resilient, e.g. **Tebilising.**
water-proofing	– or shower-proofing; garments are treated with silicone, e.g. Dri-Sil.
lustre-added	– to give a sheen to dull fabrics such as cotton, e.g. **mercerising, glazing.**

For longer life

moth-proofing	– to discourage moths in wool it can be treated with a chemical e.g. Dielmoth.
flame-proofing/ flame-resistant	– fabrics can be given a chemical process to make them 'durably flameproof' (e.g. Proban, Timonex) or the flame resistance can be built into the fibre when it is manufactured 'inherently flameproof' (e.g. Dynel, Teklan).

Example of a garment label

> Our fleece dressing gowns are made from flame-resistant modacrylic fabric for greater safety.

AQUAPERL
Easy Care

Dyed in the fabric	Crease-shy
Easy to wash	Easy to iron
Swiss fabric	100% cotton
Scotchgard	Resistant to rain, oil and dirt

Labels such as these should be attached to a garment. Many labels only tell you the type of fibres used and the washing instructions (see pp. 160 and 161).

We may find that there are some fibres and fabric finishes which we have to avoid because they are unhealthy for us.

Examples are:

Wool can irritate the skin and cause a rash, especially to babies.

Some man-made fabrics can cause allergy symptoms such as skin rashes, itching or even sneezing!

Non-porous fabrics such as PVC, rubber and elasticated fabrics do not allow perspiration to escape. They should have ventilation holes and should not be worn for long periods.

FABRICS FOR A PURPOSE

Modern clothing should suit its purpose. Scientists have helped us by giving us easy-care, easy-wear finishes but the final choice rests with you. Do not be one of those people who, when asked to go to a special occasion, always says 'I would love to come, but I haven't a thing to wear!'

1 These pictures show different groups of people and different activities. From the list of describing words on the next page, choose some which would apply to the clothing to be worn by the various groups and then explain your choice.

Babies and children

The elderly

Sporting activities

continued

*School and
working clothes*

*Night wear
and underwear*

DESCRIBING WORDS

absorbent easily-washed safe elastic cool warm
strong wind-proof comfortable flameproof loose
casual colour-fast easy-care crease-resistant
disposable inexpensive hygienic allergy-free
non-irritant soft close-fitting well-designed
stain-resistant good-looking permanently creased
hard-wearing

2 JUMBLED PAIRS

Column A shows a selection of garments and Column B
suggests different types of fabrics.

Suggest which fabric would suit which garment and
then suggest other suitable fabrics with reasons for your
choice.

Column A – *garment*	**Column B** – *fabric*
track suit	Lycra/polyester mix
baby's vest	poplin
thick sweater	PVC cotton-backed fabric
bikini	thermal fabric
man's shirt	towelling
child's nightdress	needlecord
play apron	acrylic
woman's dressing gown	wool and nylon
boy's underpants	flame-resistant wincyette
summer blouse	fleecy-backed cotton jersey
winter skirt	cotton voile
scarf and mittens	100 per cent cotton
duffle coat	quilted nylon
anorak	cotton/polyester mix

DRESS CARE

If you choose your clothes carefully they will suit their
purpose *and* suit your personality.

Be honest with yourself: are you neat, methodical, conscien-
tious and careful? OR untidy, lazy, careless and happy-go-
lucky?

A First Home Economics Course

Does your bedroom look

A *Like this?*   **B** *Like this?*

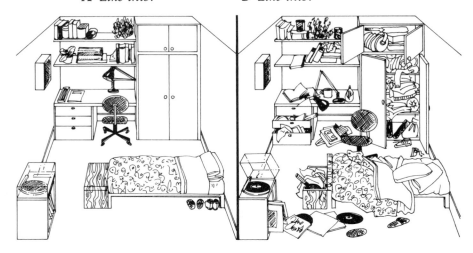

If you are type B you need all the help you can get, and so do your parents! Your clothes are going to suffer and you will never have anything unrumpled, free from holes, tears and ladders, or matching. Living like this is more trouble than it is worth.

Follow a few simple rules and the state of your dress will improve without too much effort.

CHOOSING

A   Go for the easy-care fabrics with special finishes which will not stain, crease, attract moths, shrink or lose their shape.

B   Choose simple styles with creases and pleats permanently pressed in.

C   Check that your clothes are machine-washable and minimum iron.

D   Know your care labels. Don't buy anything with this label if you can't be bothered hand washing an article.

HAND WASH

Don't buy anything with these labels if you can't afford to have garments dry cleaned.

E   Don't buy clothes if you are not certain you like them – you will probably never wear the garment and it will take up valuable storage space.

WEARING

A Don't wear garments which are too small or too tight – the seams will split and the fabric will pull into holes.

B Change out of your good clothes before cleaning your bike or weeding the garden – wear your old jeans or overalls.

C Don't put clothing away if it is dirty, smelly, damp or in need of repair, especially if it is going away until next season

D Don't think that people won't notice if your clothes are stained, have hems coming down, have holes in and are creased – they will, and they will judge you by the state of your dress.

E Remember that you can be seen from the back as well as the front. Have a mirror which shows you from all angles to avoid an awful back view.

CLEANING

A Remember that dirty clothing, especially underwear, tights and socks become smelly. They need changing and laundering regularly.

B The things you need to know about your garments are:
Will it wash or does it need dry cleaning?
Hand or machine wash?
The type of fabric.
Has it a special finish?
Might the colours run?
Does it need a long, hot wash and spin or a gentler washing action?
How is the fabric affected by heat? Will it need a hot, medium or cool iron?
You should find all this information on the care label which most garments have inside them. The back panel of a soap powder packet also illustrates all these labels.

These are pictures of all the symbols used on care labels. The left hand symbols have been left blank, the right hand symbols show examples of the instructions they may give.

Blank   Example

Washing   [95]   Very hot water may be used

continued

A First Home Economics Course

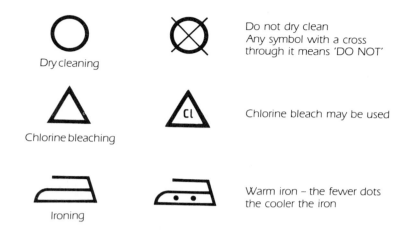

Dry cleaning

Do not dry clean
Any symbol with a cross
through it means 'DO NOT'

Chlorine bleaching

Chlorine bleach may be used

Ironing

Warm iron – the fewer dots
the cooler the iron

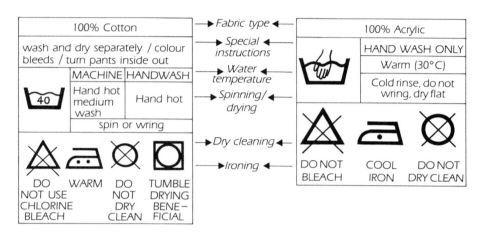

100% Cotton		
wash and dry separately / colour bleeds / turn pants inside out		
	MACHINE	HANDWASH
40	Hand hot medium wash	Hand hot
	spin or wring	

DO NOT USE CHLORINE BLEACH · WARM · DO NOT DRY CLEAN · TUMBLE DRYING BENE–FICIAL

Fabric type
Special instructions
Water temperature
Spinning/drying
Dry cleaning
Ironing

100% Acrylic		
HAND WASH ONLY		
Warm (30°C)		
Cold rinse, do not wring, dry flat		

DO NOT BLEACH · COOL IRON · DO NOT DRY CLEAN

C   Some garments are special – They may have cost you quite a lot of money. They may be very delicate, trimmed with lace or embroidery, have a special pattern or colours. They may shrink or felt in the wash. They need special care:

- wash separately – by hand
- follow any instructions on the label
- use the correct temperature of water
- use a good quality washing powder or liquid
- squeeze – do not rub
- rinse until the water is clear
- use fabric softener in the final rinse
- gently squeeze out excess water; do not twist; wrap in a towel to absorb excess moisture.
- dry by lying the garment out flat rather than using pegs
- use correct temperature for ironing.

Do a *fact finding* exercise on *washing powders*.

1 This is a selection of washing products – most people have their own favourite brands. How did they choose them?

Do a random survey, i.e. a mother with young children, a student who does his own washing, a pensioner, a children's home.

ASK

a) What types of washing powder do you use?

b) Are you pleased with your washing powder or would you like to change it?

c) How did you choose your powder?

d) Were you influenced by TV or magazine advertising?

e) Was it an impulse buy in a supermarket?

f) Was it recommended by a friend?

g) Was it the cheapest when you went to buy – on special offer or with a money-off voucher?

h) Any other reasons?

Assess your results and compare them with other members of your group.

Make a chart of the results.

2 *NOW* – compare the products yourselves. Divide into groups:

Within your group you could bring a white school blouse or shirt. Hand wash the garment using different washing products; every group using the same amount of powder.

Use
- a soap powder such as Persil or Fairy Snow
- a synthetic washing powder such as Surf or Tide
- a biological powder such as Biological Daz or Ariel.

A First Home Economics Course

If you can, wash some in an automatic washing machine using a powder especially for automatics.

Compare: ● ease of washing ● amount of lather ● number of rinses needed ● finished results (give marks out of five for each one).

Also, work out and compare the cost so that you can identify which is the best value for money.

Your chart could look something like this:

Example

(unfinished)

	Product	Ease of washing	Lather	Rinses	Finished results	Cost
Soap powder	Persil	●●●	●●			
Synthetic	Daz	●●●●	●●●●●	●●●●	●●	●●●
Biological	Ariel	●●				

Your *results* may show that: one product gives outstanding results and good value OR all products are good in some ways and poor in others.

3 You could do a similar piece of experimental work to show the value of using fabric conditioners.

D The condition of a person's dress is usually a good guide to their personality. Badly *stained* garments indicate a sloppy dresser; even a few stains can spoil a whole outfit. If you are a rather messy person it is sensible to:

● buy clothes with stain-resistant qualities
● avoid stains by:
    wearing old clothes for dirty jobs
    using an apron when cooking, etc.
    using a napkin when eating.

For those stains which do appear there are a few basic rules:

● identify the stain and the type of fabric
● tackle the stain immediately – if it is allowed to 'set' in it will be more difficult to remove
● blot up as much of the stain as possible, dab with cold water – do not rub as this spreads the stain
● try simple methods first such as washing or soaking, depending upon the type of fabric. Many stains will respond to washing and/or soaking in an enzyme washing powder
● if possible try out any stain remover on a hidden part first (e.g. the hem or seam allowance) – it could damage the fabric

- keep some commercial brands of stain removers in the home for emergencies, Thawpit and Stain Devils are very efficient
- some stain-removing agents are dangerous – see they are labelled and kept out of reach of children
- for stains on delicate or precious articles seek professional advice.

STORING

A   No matter how tired you are, always hang your clothes up – creases in garments which have just been dropped on the floor may not come out.

B   Try to have some method about storing your clothing. Fold things neatly and put them in their proper place.

C   Use padded coat hangers for soft fabrics and special hangers for skirts and trousers.

D   Do not put dirty or stained clothing away, it will smell and make the rest of your clothing smell unpleasant. It will also attract moths.

E   Store winter and summer clothes separately when not in use, check them and clean them before storage.

F   Do not keep garments which you never wear, they just clutter up your storage space.

G   Clean and/or polish shoes and boots before storage. Shoe trees will help to keep them in good shape.

Storage space is usually limited especially if you have to share with a brother or sister. Here are some good ideas which could help you to make the most of the space available.

Storage ideas

Open cubby-holes for storing tights, socks, pullovers, books, writing equipment, jewellery

Office-type equipment
or kitchen vegetable
racks make good, cheap
accessible storage for
clothing, books etc

Shoe rack attached to
cupboard door

Floor to ceiling shelving
gives plenty of room for
books, school projects
or bulky clothing

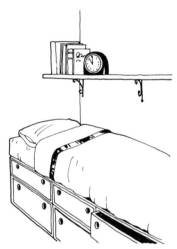

Use the space below
and above your bed for
storage

Strong cardboard fruit
boxes or cartons stacked
together hold shoes

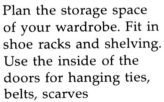

Plan the storage space
of your wardrobe. Fit in
shoe racks and shelving.
Use the inside of the
doors for hanging ties,
belts, scarves

Draw a plan of your own bedroom or a bedroom you would like to have. Show the position of the furniture. Draw the plan to scale. Make a list of all the items of clothing, books and equipment which need storing and describe how and where you would put everything.

You can get ideas from magazines, furniture brochures and catalogues.

REPAIRING

Clothes used to be made and bought to last. Styles did not change quickly and clothing tended to be strong and well-made. Much of our present day clothing is 'fashion wear' and will be replaced from year to year.

We expect some of our clothing to last; things like school uniform, nightwear, socks and topcoats. These should be well-made in suitable fabrics with special finishes and often they will be outgrown before they are outworn.

Repairing garments can be a tedious job, but it is necessary if you don't wish to look untidy and careless.

There is a difference between looking:

casual – like this   OR   *messy* – like this

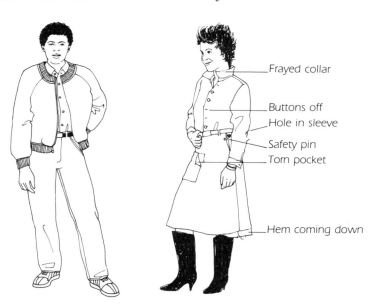

Frayed collar

Buttons off
Hole in sleeve

Safety pin
Torn pocket

Hem coming down

Repairs can be kept to a minimum by following a few basic rules:

A 'A stitch in time saves nine' – this saying explains itself!

B Small repair jobs will grow quickly into large ones and safety pins will only cause more wear and tear.

C Do check regularly that buttons are safely secured. Losing one button may mean replacing a whole set if you can't get another to match.

D Use matching yarn for your repairs. A 'near miss' could look worse than the tear or hole. Sometimes you can pull a thread from the fabric to use.

E Some garments supply spare buttons and/or matching thread. Always keep some if you make the garment yourself.

F Use your sewing machine to do repairs. The finished result will be stronger and neater. Learn how to machine darn.

G The worn area around a hole will also need repairing. You may be able to reinforce it with iron-on Vilene.

H Don't waste time repairing garments which are very old and worn or too small. It may be better to use the best parts to create another garment e.g. make shorts from trousers or a pinafore dress from a dress.

I If you really cannot bear patching, darning or mending, or the damaged area is very large, make a feature of it. Try a ready made iron-on patch in contrasting fabric or replace a torn pocket with different fabric. Appliqué motifs, stuck or sewn on, will cover most worn areas. Hems can be ironed in place with Wonda-web.

J Danger – some worn areas not only look messy but can be dangerous, e.g. torn cuffs, down-at-heel shoes, broken fasteners. Valuables can be lost through holes in pockets.

It is harder to feel self-confident if you know you have laddered tights, a hole in your sock or buttons missing – MEND IT.

REVISION – DRESS QUIZ

Fashion

1. What does 'mix and match' mean in your choice of clothes?

2. Do you think it is worthwhile to know how to:
   i) make your own clothes
   ii) alter your own clothes
   iii) repair your own clothes?

3. In this country it is traditional for a bridal gown to be white. Find out about the wedding traditions in other countries and religions.

4. A teenage fashion magazine is running a competition for 'Young New Designers'. Design and write a brief account of a garment or an outfit which you would like a top Fashion House to produce for you as the first prize in the competition.

5. Hats are often worn as part of a national costume or religion. Name some examples and try to find some illustrations.

6. Find out how a 'consumer' is protected by the Sale of Goods Act.

7. 'Clothes are like a second skin.' Look for other sayings related to our appearance and dress and briefly explain what you think is meant by each one e.g. 'Beauty is only skin deep', 'do not judge a book by its cover'.

8. Describe the points you would look for when trying on a new garment to see if it is a good fit.

9. Accessories (e.g. bows, belts) may be added to enhance the appearance of clothes. Make a list of accessories currently in fashion and state when they should be worn.

10. Why is it to your advantage to choose colours which complement your natural colouring?

A First Home Economics Course

Dress sense

1. What do we mean when we say that 'clothing should suit its purpose'?

2. Suggest five things to be considered when buying clothing suitable for school wear.

3. Put the word 'durable' into a sentence to explain its meaning.

4. Write a paragraph each about two natural fibres and two man-made fibres.

5. Name the fibres associated with the following words:
   ● worm ● coal ● flax ● boll ● wood ● sheep.

6. Which of the words in brackets is the correct answer?
   Silk is a very (smooth, rough, heavy) fabric.
   A filament is a (type of needle, a cotton plant, a continuous fibre).
   It is the (stem, flower, husk) of the flax plant which is used to make linen.
   Plying means to (knit, twist threads together, wind on to a bobbin).
   Linen is (stronger than, weaker than, about the same strength as) cotton.
   A silkworm can spin a continuous thread up to (1 metre, 10 metres, 2 km) long.
   Artificial silk was first shown in (1760, 1880, 1950).
   Woollen fibre can be made into yarn by using (a loom, a hopper, a spinning wheel).

7. Name two useful properties associated with the following:
   ● cotton ● wool ● polyester ● nylon.

8. What are the benefits of a fabric made from a blend of polyester and cotton?

9. Name special finishes which can be applied to garments to help them to:
   ● last longer ● wear better ● look better ● be safer ● be easier to care for.

10. What is meant by: a non-woven fabric ● a non-porous fabric?

Dress care

1. How will you know if garments:
   - need hand washing • need dry cleaning?

2. What could be the possible results of putting clothing away damp?

3. Name three things which a care label will tell you.

4. Give at least three general instructions for the laundering of delicate fabrics.

5. Would you always buy the washing powder which was on special offer? Why?

6. Why do we sometimes use fabric conditioner?

7. How would you deal with:
   - a tea stain on a linen cloth
   - a butter stain on a cotton dress
   - a Biro mark on Terylene trousers?

8. Describe or draw the best type of clothes hangers for:
   - a soft woollen garment
   - a pair of trousers
   - a pleated skirt.

9. Describe the treatment for a pair of damp, muddy leather shoes.

10. Give five reasons for keeping clothes in good repair.

CONCLUSION
Fitting the pieces together

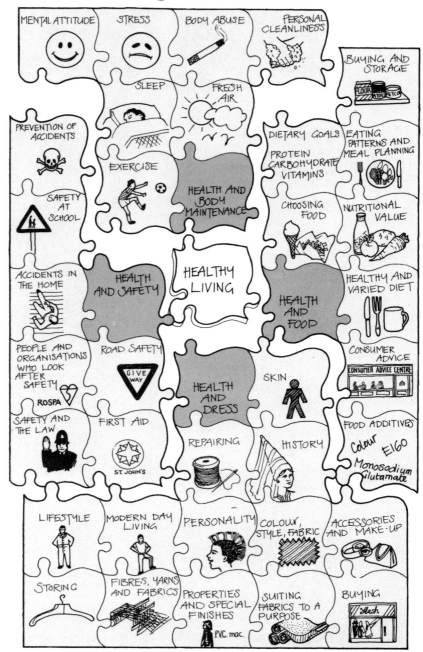

Have *you* solved the healthy living puzzle?

When all these parts of the jigsaw are fitted together, you get a complete picture of the basics needed for healthy living.

It takes hard work to achieve and then maintain these standards and only *you* can do it – but in the end it is well worthwhile – you will **LOOK BETTER** and **FEEL BETTER**.

Glossary

Some of the terms used in this book.

ANALYSE
• to examine facts and situations in detail and record the results

CALORIE
• a measurement of heat energy, for example as food is digested

CONSUMER
• a person who acquires or buys and uses goods

CONTAGIOUS
• infectious

CULTURE
• ideas and activities of a group resulting from social, racial and economic background

DIET
• the food we eat everyday; a special selection of food for certain health conditions

DIGESTION
• the process of breaking down food into its various nutrients and their absorption into the body

DURABILITY
• resistance to wear

EEC
• European Economic Community (the Common Market countries)

ENZYME
• chemical which occurs in living things to speed up chemical processes

ETHNIC
• belonging to customs, dress, food, etc. of a racial group

EVALUATE
• to decide the value or use of something

FAMILY COMMITMENT
• measure of loyalty within a family

FOETUS
• the unborn baby in the womb after its parts are distinctly formed until its birth

HAUTE COUTURE
• high class fashion

INFANT MORTALITY RATE
• the number of infant deaths in the first year of life per 1000 live births

KILOJOULE
• see calorie

LOGO
• identifying badge or symbol

MANUAL WORKER
• someone who does hard physical work, e.g. bricklayer.

MATURITY
• degree of adulthood

MENSTRUATION	●	the female cycle which results in monthly shedding of an egg and the lining of the womb, 'periods'
NEGATIVE FEELINGS	●	bad or ill feelings
NOTIFIABLE ACCIDENT	●	accidents which must be reported, by law
NUTRITION	●	the study of nutrients in food
OPTICAL ILLUSIONS	●	things which are not as they appear
PASSIVE SMOKING	●	inhaling smoke from other people's tobacco
PERSONAL APPRAISAL	●	self assessment
PHOBIAS	●	irrational or unreasonable fears
POSITIVE FEELINGS	●	good and sympathetic feelings
SEDENTARY WORKER	●	someone whose work involves a lot of sitting, e.g. office worker
STATUTORY	●	legal or by law
STATUS SYMBOL	●	an article or possession intended to display a person's position in their social group
STIMULANT	●	a substance which tends to increase or excite activity
THERAPY	●	treatment, aimed at easing a medical condition
VOLUNTARY	●	acting by choice, without compulsion
YARN	●	any type of spun thread

INDEX

Items listed in the Contents are not included in the Index unless the reference is to an Activity. All Activities have a **bold** page reference.

Accessories, choosing **143**
Accidents
  cost of 88
  first aid for 91
  in home 54–5, **55**
  reaction to (role-play) **94**
  road 64–73, **66–8, 70–71**
  survey of **55–6, 63–4**
Additives 125, **126**
Adrenaline 28
Adult, diet of **112**
Air 21–2, **23**
Alcohol, drinking 30–7, **33, 35**
Amino acids 99
Athletes, success of **10**

Bacteria 46, 119
Balance skills 6
Bedbug 47–9
Body abuse 5, 30–7
Burns 54

Calcium 100, 108, 111, 113
Calories (K cal) 108
Carbohydrates 98–9, 108, 111, 113
Carbon dioxide 22
Children
  diet of **110–11**
  play of **6**
Choking 54
Cleanliness, personal 39–51
Clothing
  analysis of **135–6**
  assessment of **145**
  storage of **166**
Colour
  of clothing **136**
  personal **137**
Colourings (foods) 125
Consumer
  Safety Act (1978) 89
  survey **44–5**
Convenience foods 106, **106**
Cotton 146–7

Danger, awareness of **57–8, 61, 83**
Diet 96, **102–3, 104**, 111–15
  modified 116
Disease 96
Dreams 24
Dress, study of historic **132–3**
Drugs illegal 30–9, **33, 35**

Elderly
  diet of **114**
  road safety and 77, **77**
Enzyme 119
Exercise, physical 7, 8, **8, 9, 11, 18**, 19–20
Expectant mother, diet of **113**
Extended family 1

Fabric **140**, 149, 152–8, **152, 155, 157**
Falls 54
Family **2, 3**
  hygiene 46
Fashion design **139**
Fast food **105, 109**
Fats 99–100, 108, 111, 113
Fatty acids 100
Fibre (dietary) 98, 108, 113
Fibre (fabric) **148**, 156
  animal 146, 147, 148
  vegetable 146, 147, 148
  man-made 146, 147, 148
First aid
  procedures 92–3
  sporting injuries and **20**
Flavourings 125
Flax 146, 147
Fleas 47–9
Food
  buying **116–7, 119**
  labelling **122**, 123, **124–5**
  storage 119, **120–21**

Glazing, fabric 156
Green Cross Code 68

Hand/eye coordination 6
Health, damage to **4**
Health and Safety at Work Act (1974) 80
Health and Safety Officer 81
Health Education Authority 12, 88
Heart beat 15–17
Human body, efficiency 13
Hygiene, personal 39–51, **40, 44–6**

Improvers 125
Infant, diet of **110**
Intellectual development 6
Invalid, diet of **114–5**
Iron 108, 111

Kitemark 60
Knitting **151**

Law, and safety 88–9, **90**
Labels, on garments 159–61
Lice 47–9
Linen 146, 147
Long house 128

Make-up, experimenting with **144**
Malnutrition 96
Mental attitudes 51–3
Mercerising 156
Micro-organisms 119
Minerals 98–100, 111, 113, 115
Mite 47–9
Mordant 156
Mould 119
Muscular skills 6

Nitrogen 21–2
Nuclear family 2
Nutrients 97–100, **97**, **101**, 108
Nylon 147

Olympic Games **10**
Oxygen 21–2

Personal profile **41–2**
Play (and development) **6**
Poisoning 54, 62
Preservatives 125
Protein 98–9, 108, 111, 114
Pulse rate 15, **16–17**

Rapid eye movement (REM) 23–4
Recommended daily allowances (RDA) 107
Regenerated fibres 147
Road safety
    children 66–7
    cyclists 72
    elderly 77, **77**
    equipment 76
    motorcyclists 72
    motorists 73
    pedestrians 71
    posters **79**
    signs **68**
Round worm 49
Royal Society for the Prevention of Accidents
    (RoSPA) 55, 88

'S' factor **15**
Safety
    careers in **87–8**
    equipment **59**
    labels **60**
    wear **81–2**
Sanforising 156
Scabies 48, 49
Scalds 54
Silk 146–7
Skin, structure of 47
Sleep 23–7, **25**, 111
Smoking 30–7, **33**, **35**
Social skills 6
Spinning **150**
Sports Council 9–11
Sport
    injury **20–1**
    participation in **6**, 7, 9–11, **12**, 14
    reporting of **12**
Stamina 14
Starvation 96
Strength 14
Stress 7, 27–9, **29**
Suffocation 54
Suppleness 14
Synthetic fibre 147

Tape worm 49
Tebilising 156
Teenager, diet of **111**
Tepee 128
Thread worm 49
Trubenising 156

Vegan 115
Vegetarian, diet of **115**
Vitamins 98–100, 111, 114, 115
    vitamin A 100
    B 100, 113
    C 100, 108
    D 22, 100, 113
    E 100
    K 100

Washing products, fabrics **162–3**
Water
    in diet 98
    safety 84, **85–6**
Weaving **150**
Wool 146–7
Worms, parasitic 49

Yarn 148–9
Yeast 119